Table of Contents

P9-DZM-895

All terms appearing in boldfaced type in the text are defined in the Glossary on pages 78 to 80.

Aziza was very excited about her presentation topic, "Digging Up the Past." She had borrowed the sand table from Ms. Adachi's kindergarten classroom for her demonstration. She planned to show her classmates how an archaeologist excavates, or digs up, the past. Before the presentation, Aziza buried pieces of a broken vase and plate in the sand. During her presentation, Aziza would carefully scrape away the sand to uncover each buried object. This would be the best presentation she had ever done.

Archaeologists are scientists who study ancient peoples and the way they lived. They are like detectives who try to uncover, or dig up, the past.

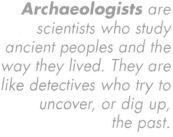

These artifacts were discovered by archaeologists. What do you think they are, and what do they tell you about the lives of the people who made and used them?

ARCHAEOLOGY

To study ancient peoples and the times during which they lived, it is helpful to understand certain words that are used throughout this book. **History** is the study of the past, and **archaeology** is part of it. Archaeology is the study of human history through **excavation**, or the digging up of remains or ancient **artifacts**.

Artifacts are objects that were made by people, and they can include coins, pottery, tools, clothing, and buildings. They can provide information about a people's **culture**. Culture is a way of life; it includes the food people eat, the clothes they wear, and the music they listen to. It also includes their language, religion, and government.

Less than 100 years ago, archaeologists did not follow a scientific method of gathering information. They often destroyed important artifacts as they dug through a site, or an area, or blew it up with dynamite. More valuable items, such as jewellery, pottery, furniture, or weapons, were placed in museums or sold to individuals. Other artifacts, such as tools, buildings, clothing, vehicles, and artwork were thrown away or destroyed and are therefore lost forever. Today archaeologists know that even a small piece of pottery may hold a clue that will help us to understand a group of people and its culture. They carefully excavate, or dig, through the site and identify, label, and describe the remains or artifacts that they find. Later they clean and assemble these objects, taking great care not to damage them. Some ancient artifacts and remains must be treated with chemicals so that they do not decay while being studied. Human remains, plants, wood, and metals all decompose, or break down, when exposed to air and bacteria.

DATING THE PAST

It is important to understand when historical events occurred. A **timeline** is a line that shows important dates and events in history and can be used to show the development of a civilization.

Over the ages, different methods have been used to date time. To indicate a particular year in time, archaeologists and historians have started to use the terms **BCE** and **CE**. CE stands for Common Era, which includes all years after, and including, year 1. BCE stands for Before the Common Era. These terms are replacing the older terms of BC and AD.

The civilization of the ancient Maya lasted from 1000 BCE to 1546 CE. When did the civilization of ancient Greece begin? Approximately when did it end?

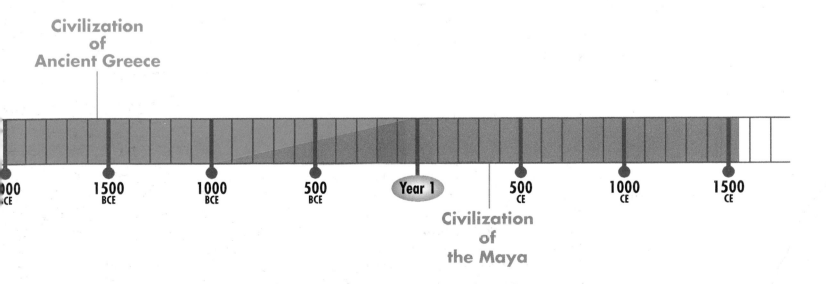

Civilization of Ancient Greece

2000 BCE | 1500 BCE | 1000 BCE | 500 BCE | Year 1 | 500 CE | 1000 CE | 1500 CE

Civilization of the Maya

Early Civilizations

CIVILIZATION

Before 8000 BCE, people were **nomadic**. Nomadic is the word we use to describe people who travel across the land hunting and gathering food. These groups of people used tools made from stone, bone, or wood and dug pits or built huts for shelter. Between 8000 and 5000 BCE, people discovered that they could produce their own food by planting crops. During this time, they also realized that they could **domesticate**, or tame, animals, such as pigs, sheep, and goats, which they used for food. This important time period is called the **Neolithic Age**.

The discovery of **agriculture**, or farming, increased people's food supply and made it possible for them to live together in permanent settlements. Over time, people formed different civilizations. **Civilization** comes from the Latin word *civis*, meaning "citizen" or "a person who lives in a city." Living together in permanent settlements, such as villages, towns, or cities, gave people time to improve farming techniques, trade, develop religious beliefs, form governments, produce art, create a written language, and make scientific discoveries. These are features of a civilization.

The civilizations we will investigate in this book are believed to be some of the oldest civilizations on earth. They existed, wholly or in part, Before the Common Era (BCE). Some have been studied by archaeologists for many years, and a lot of information about them has been uncovered. Others have only recently been explored

An artist's interpretation showing changes from a nomadic to a settled society.

Nomadic peoples travelled from place to place hunting animals and gathering wild plants for food.

People discovered that if they planted seeds, they could grow their own plants for food. They also realized that they could round up animals and keep them in enclosures to provide meat and milk.

People no longer had to travel from place to place looking for food. They formed permanent settlements.

by archaeologists and remain somewhat of a mystery. As archaeologists continue to investigate these early civilizations, we will gain a better understanding of them and our world.

SOMETHING TO DO

1. Working in small groups, play the role of archaeologists by piecing together a broken artifact, such as a plate, pot, or mug. Make sure to clean, identify, label, describe, and assemble your artifact.

2. List five possessions, or artifacts, that you would leave behind to help future archaeologists understand the way you lived. Bring your artifacts to class, and explain why you chose them.

3. a) Explain the meaning of *civilization*.

   b) Create a web, like the one showing features of a civilization on this page, to show features of culture.

4. Create a timeline to show the important events in your life. The timeline should begin on the year that you were born.

5. To find out more about ancient artifacts and remains, plan a trip to a museum that contains exhibits on early civilizations. During your visit, take notes about the objects that are displayed. Create a brochure describing the exhibit to others. Illustrate your brochure.

Where did the world's first civilization appear? Archaeologists believe that the world's first civilization appeared in Mesopotamia. *Mesopotamia* is a Greek word that means "the land between the rivers." This name was given to the communities that began to appear between the Tigris and Euphrates rivers around 3500 BCE. These two rivers are found in an area of the world that was called the **Fertile Crescent**. It was an arch-shaped band of land that stretched from the Persian Gulf to the Mediterranean Sea. The Fertile Crescent included parts of countries we know today as Kuwait, Iraq, Israel, Lebanon, Jordan, and Syria.

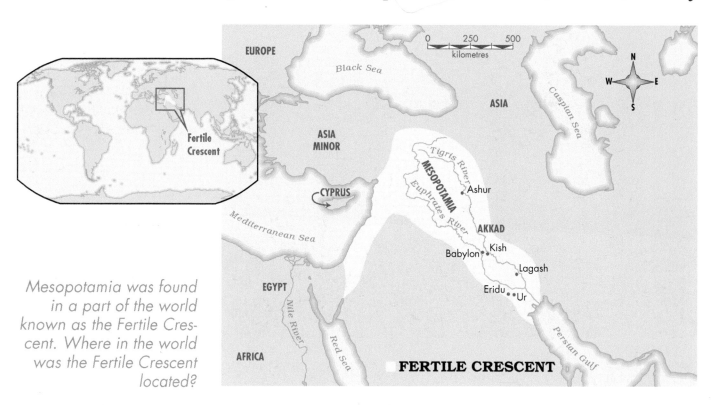

Mesopotamia was found in a part of the world known as the Fertile Crescent. Where in the world was the Fertile Crescent located?

LAND AND CLIMATE

Ancient Mesopotamia lay between the Tigris and Euphrates rivers. The climate was hot and dry in the summer; it was mild and wet in the winter. **Climate** is the weather conditions that occur in an area over a long period of time.

Around 3500 BCE, people started to settle along the **flood plains** of the Tigris and Euphrates rivers. A flood plain is a low, flat area of land beside a river that can be flooded during the year. The fertile land of Mesopotamia, which was nourished by the yearly flooding of the Tigris and Euphrates rivers, provided a good place for people to settle. The northern region of Mesopotamia received plenty of rainfall, which helped crops grow. There was less rainfall in the southern region, but the fertile soil left by the flood waters of the Tigris and Euphrates rivers produced good farmland.

The marshes and wetlands of the southern region contained many fish and birds. The rich soil of the Fertile Crescent provided a good environment for the growth of grasses in the plains and trees in the more rocky areas. Many wild animals lived on these lands, including elephants, gazelles, antelopes, cattle, boars, wolves, donkeys, sheep, goats, and lions. People who lived in the area began to farm by tilling the soil and domesticating animals. They domesticated animals by taming them and using them for food, clothing, and hunting.

The ancient Mesopotamians are believed to be some of the first people to grow crops and domesticate animals. Their development of agriculture, or farming, led to the formation of the first villages, towns, and cities. The people of Mesopotamia grew forms of wheat and barley to make food and drink, such as bread and beer. Crops and herds of animals became plentiful, which helped civilizations to prosper in the area.

As the Mesopotamians learned to control the flooding of the Tigris and Euphrates rivers, drain the land, and water the soil, they began to produce excellent crops.

DID YOU KNOW?

The date palm was so important to the people of this region that it appeared on many of their artifacts, including pottery, sculptures, seals or stamps, and other objects.

Date palms grow well in the saltwater wetlands along the Tigris and Euphrates rivers. The Mesopotamians developed hundreds of uses for this tree. They ate its fruit and used its leaves, bark, and wood to make tools, clothing, and homes.

Natural Environment

GEOGRAPHIC FEATURES

Maps can show the location of physical and human features. **Physical features** are created by nature. Some examples are rivers, marshes, mountains, deserts, lakes, and oceans. **Human features** are created by people. Some examples are roads, cities, and country borders. Often the location of human features, such as roads and cities, has been affected by physical features. Symbols and colours are used on maps to represent physical and human features. The explanation of these symbols is given in the legend.

This map of today's world shows the area that used to be ancient Mesopotamia.

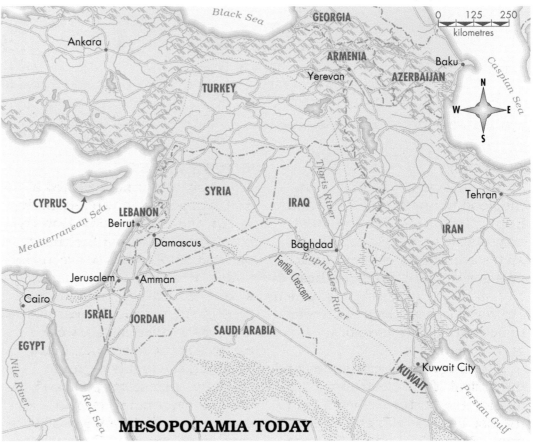

MESOPOTAMIA TODAY

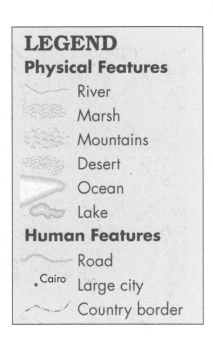

LEGEND

Physical Features

- River
- Marsh
- Mountains
- Desert
- Ocean
- Lake

Human Features

- Road
- Cairo   Large city
- Country border

SOMETHING TO DO

1. Describe the land and climate of ancient Mesopotamia. Why was it a good place to settle?

2. How was agriculture important to the growth of Mesopotamia?

3. Refer to the map on page 6 to draw and colour the Fertile Crescent on an outline map showing the area of ancient Mesopotamia today. Indicate the following features: Tigris River, Euphrates River, and Mediterranean Sea.

4. Look at the map on this page, and answer the following questions:

   a) In which country do the Euphrates and Tigris rivers meet?

   b) Name a city in each of the following countries: Syria, Iran, and Iraq.

   c) Name three seas.

   d) Beside which physical feature are most cities located? Give reasons for this.

   e) Are there many human features in desert or marsh areas? Explain.

Society and Culture

3500–1900 BCE
Sumerian Civilization
Farming towns along the banks of the Tigris and Euphrates rivers become the Sumerian city-states of Ur, Eridu, Kish, Lagash, and Babylon.

1300–609 BCE
Assyrian Civilization
The Assyrians take control of Babylonia and all of Mesopotamia.

| 3500 BCE | 3000 BCE | 2500 BCE | 2000 BCE | 1500 BCE | 1000 BCE | 500 BCE |

1900–1300 BCE
Babylonian Civilization
Invaders from the west, called Amorites, settle in Babylon. Under the leadership of King Hammurabi, they form the empire of Babylonia.

609–530 BCE
Chaldean Civilization
Chaldeans rule Mesopotamia. King Nebuchadnezzar turns Babylon into one of the most beautiful cities in the world.

HISTORY

As people started to settle along the flood plains of the Tigris and Euphrates rivers, the first great **city-states** were formed. City-states are large cities with their own government. Many of these city-states became empires, which are very large settlements under the control of a person or a government.

Fighting among city-states and the arrival of invaders from outside the Fertile Crescent led to the rise and fall of many civilizations. From 3500 BCE to 530 BCE, Mesopotamia was ruled by four major civilizations: the Sumerians, the Babylonians, the Assyrians, and the Chaldeans. The Babylonians created one of the first written codes of law. They were also one of the first peoples to use money. The Chaldean king Nebuchadnezzar built the Hanging Gardens of Babylon, which is one of the seven wonders of the ancient world.

GOVERNMENT

The early Sumerians elected a group of people, or an assembly, to run the **government**. Government is what we call the ruling of a nation. As wars between city-states became more frequent, strong leaders were needed to protect the people. The early kings of Sumer, called *lugals*, were elected by the assembly. Later, however, the lugals began to consider themselves gods and handed over their power to members of their family when they grew too old to rule. Because the people believed that their king was a god, the governments of the Mesopotamian civilizations were considered theocracies. A **theocracy** is a form of government led by a god or religious figure.

In Mesopotamia, the lugals provided military leadership and protection, oversaw building projects, and established laws. Later, city-states were divided into provinces, which were ruled by governors.

To create the Hanging Gardens of Babylon, King Nebuchadnezzar had workers construct a building with several terraces on the palace grounds. On each terrace, they planted magnificent gardens, which included flowers, vines, flowering trees, and shrubs.

Mesopotamia

DID YOU KNOW?

Homes in Mesopotamia were built so close together that people could travel across the flat rooftops and enter by climbing down a ladder through a hole in the ceiling.

SOCIAL STRUCTURE

Lugals had control over their city-state or empire and owned all the land and buildings within it. Priests were in charge of giving out land to the farmers and running the schools. **Scribes** were public writers who worked for religious temples or the government.

Craftspeople made products that traders sold locally and in other parts of the world. The common people, who were usually farmers, made up most of the population. Slaves were either prisoners of war or people who desperately needed money and sold themselves into slavery.

FAMILY LIFE

Family life was considered very important in Mesopotamian society. The father was the head of the family and had complete control over his children. Women were highly respected and could own land or property, as well as establish their own business; however, they could not vote or govern.

Boys of wealthy families started going to school at the age of eight or nine. School ran from sun-up to sunset, and discipline was strict. Students were punished if their work was not perfect. They learned to read and write, and they studied mathematics, science, history, and geography. Common people could not afford to go to school and were trained at home or in workshops. The boys learned specific trades, such as pottery-making, metalwork, or woodwork, while the girls were taught to run a household. Parents chose whom their children would marry.

In Mesopotamian society, priests were respected because religion was very important in the people's lives. Scribes were respected because they were the only people who could read and write.

lugal (king)

priests

scribes

traders and craftspeople

common people

slaves

In Sumerian schools, students sat in rows of benches made of mud bricks. They wrote their school work on clay tablets. Archaeologists have found many clay tablets with teachers' corrections on them.

RELIGIOUS BELIEFS

Gods and Goddesses

The ancient Mesopotamians believed in many gods and goddesses. This belief in many gods is called **polytheism**. The Mesopotamians believed that every element of the natural and human world was controlled and protected by a god or goddess. These elements included the seasons, the harvest, and war.

Because people believed that these gods were responsible for everything that occurred on earth, it was important to try to understand the gods and what they wanted. The Mesopotamians believed that the king could communicate directly with a god or goddess and that priests could try to understand the wishes of a god by performing special religious ceremonies. Many people sought out **oracles**—people believed to have special powers that helped them determine the wishes of the gods. The Mesopotamians believed that their gods had human characteristics and personalities: they got married, had children, and needed to eat and drink.

The Mesopotamians believed that their gods lived in the heavens and that when they visited the earth, they lived in a **ziggurat**. A ziggurat is a mountain-shaped temple with a pyramid-shaped base and a shrine, or place of worship, on top. Ziggurats were built by the Sumerians to house their gods while they visited the earth. They were made of thousands of sun-dried bricks. Because mud bricks weather badly, little remains of the ancient ziggurats today.

Enki
God of Earth and Water

Ninhursag
Mother Goddess of All Living Things

Enki and Ninhursag were two of the most important Mesopotamian gods.

SOMETHING TO DO

1. a) Describe the role of the following people in Mesopotamian society: lugal, priests, traders and craftspeople, and common people.

    b) If you had lived in ancient Mesopotamia, which role would you like to have had? Why?

2. The Hanging Gardens of Babylon are one of the seven wonders of the ancient world.

    a) Pretend that you are living in Mesopotamia around 600 BCE and have just visited this ancient wonder. Write a short letter to a friend describing what you saw.

    b) Use books, magazines, or the Internet to research the other wonders of the ancient world. Select one, and create a poster about it to present to the class.

3. Design a ziggurat for either the god Enki or the goddess Ninhursag. Draw your ziggurat on a piece of paper, and make sure it reflects what the god or goddess represents.

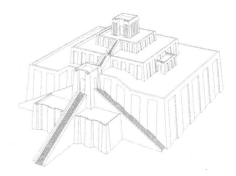

This illustration shows a ziggurat.

 esopotamia has often been called the "cradle of civilization." The Mesopotamians are believed to be among the first peoples to grow crops, form towns, and create city-states. Many of the achievements of the Mesopotamians contributed to the development of later civilizations. The invention of the wheel is considered one of the most important contributions of the Mesopotamians to the world.

THE WHEEL

The Mesopotamians were the first people to use the wheel, which was invented by the Sumerians. The invention of the wheel changed human life on earth. Wagons and chariots could be used to transport people and heavy loads, such as crop harvests and other products. Before the invention of the wheel, heavy loads were carried by people or donkeys.

Wheels were also used in pulleys to raise water from wells. The potter's wheel made it possible for people to make containers, such as vases, urns, and drinking vessels.

This Mesopotamian work of art, called the *Standard of Ur*, was made around 2700 BCE. It is the earliest artifact ever discovered showing a wheel.

Yoke

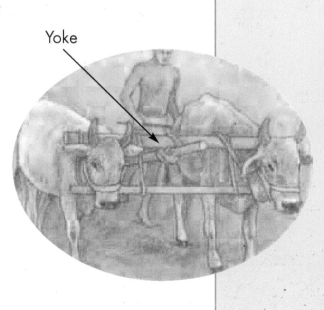

AGRICULTURE

Since Mesopotamian society was based on agriculture, it is no surprise that the Mesopotamians invented many farming tools and techniques. One technique was the use of the yoke to attach animals, such as oxen, to their plows. The Mesopotamians also invented plows that turned the soil and drilled holes into the ground to plant seeds. Their most important farming inventions were in the area of **irrigation**, which is the watering of land. The Mesopotamians built a system of dams, which are barriers that hold back water. They also built canals, or waterways, to control the movement of water. Irrigation was very important because it allowed the Mesopotamians to farm dry land and grow more crops. This illustration shows how Mesopotamian farmers used the yoke to help them plow their fields.

MONEY AND TRADE

Craftspeople, such as potters, carpenters, weavers, and metal workers, produced goods that people could use and trade. They made products such as clothing, farming tools, bowls, and jewellery. Merchants travelled on ships and small boats to trade these products, along with raw materials such as wool, barley, and wheat. They traded their goods with people in other parts of the world for items such as ivory, wood, and stone.

The Babylonians were among the first peoples to trade money for goods. The *shekel* was a coin made, most often, of silver. It weighed the same as 180 grains of barley, which was the most important grain in Mesopotamia. Another coin, called a *mina*, was worth 60 shekels, and a *talent* was worth 60 minas. This illustration shows how Babylonian money might have looked.

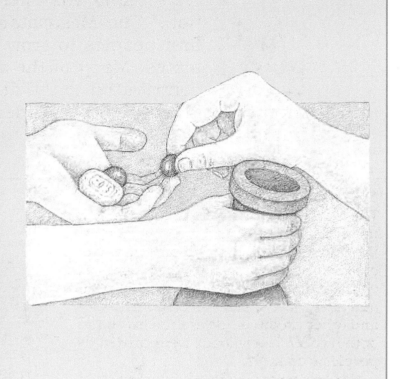

WRITING

As far as we know, the Mesopotamians were the first people to develop written language. Their writing started as picture words and developed into **cuneiform**. Cuneiform is a system of symbols that represent objects and ideas. These symbols were carved on clay tablets to record information about trade, mathematics, and law, as well as other things. Over time, the picture words were simplified into symbols, and then into strokes, so that they could be written more quickly.

	3300 BCE	2800 BCE	2400 BCE	1800 BCE
Mountain				
Grain				
Ox				
Bird				

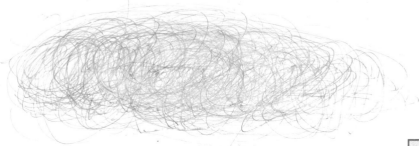

SCIENCE AND MATHEMATICS

Many of the ancient cuneiform tablets that archaeologists have found are medical prescriptions. The cuneiform tablet in this photograph is thought to be the oldest known medical text. In Mesopotamia, medical treatment involved an *ashipu*, or sorcerer, and an *asu*, or physician. The ashipu treated ailments with charms and spells to appease the gods. The asu cleaned and bandaged wounds, prepared casts, and performed surgery.

In the area of astronomy, the Mesopotamians observed the movement of the sun, moon, and stars. They used this information to predict later movements. Some stars were grouped together to form signs of the zodiac. These groups of stars were given a name, meaning, and shape. People used these groups of stars to predict the future, a practice used by astrologers today.

The Mesopotamians used mathematics to build canals, keep farm and trade records, and calculate the amount of taxes that people owed to the government. Their mathematics system was based on the number 60. Mesopotamians were able to perform both simple and complex mathematical problems using this system. Some of the mathematics that we use today is based on this system. We use the 360-degree circle, the 60-minute hour, and the 60-second minute.

METALWORK

Mesopotamians worked with many metals to create jewellery, tools, and weapons. At first, they used copper, which is a soft metal that could be used for making jewellery but is not strong enough to make tools and weapons. Most historians believe that the Mesopotamians were the first in the world to use **bronze**, around 3000 BCE. Bronze is a stronger metal, made by mixing copper and tin, which the people used to make tools and weapons. Iron was introduced to the Mesopotamians by the Hittites, a warrior tribe from present-day Turkey that invaded Babylonia around 1595 BCE. It was used to create stronger tools and weapons.

LAW

Some of the most important contributions of the Mesopotamians to the world were their laws. Their most important set of laws was created by Hammurabi, the king of Babylonia who ruled around 1792 BCE. His code included 282 laws about matters such as family life, work, buying and selling land, and trade.

Hammurabi's Code

> If a noble destroys the eye of another noble, his eye shall be destroyed.

> If a noble has committed robbery and has been caught, he shall be put to death.

> If a man has rented his boat to a boatman, and if the boatman is careless and destroys the boat, the boatman will have to give a boat to the owner in compensation.

> If a doctor performs an operation that causes death or injury to a noble, his hand shall be cut off.

> If a son strikes his father, his hand shall be cut off.

SOMETHING TO DO

1. a) The wheel was a very important invention. How did it help the people of Mesopotamia?

   b) Name at least five uses of the wheel within your school or home.

2. Create a chart like the one below to name three Mesopotamian achievements, identify why they were important, and explain how they have been changed for use in today's world.

Achievement	Importance	Today's World

3. If you had a medical emergency, would you prefer to be treated by an *ashipu* or an *asu*? Explain your choice.

4. Read each of the laws of Hammurabi shown above. Identify whether you think each law is fair or too harsh. If you think the law is too harsh, write a fairer law to replace it. Be prepared to share your opinions with the class.

5. Working in a small group, select one of the laws of Hammurabi and debate its fairness with another group. One group should try to prove that the law is fair, while the other should discuss why it is unfair.

3 Egypt

When you think of Egypt, images of mummies, pyramids, and pharaohs probably come to mind. These and other mysteries of ancient Egypt have fascinated people throughout the centuries. The Egyptian civilization began around 3100 BCE along the longest river in the world—the **Nile**. By the fertile banks of the Nile, Egypt developed into one of the most important civilizations that the world has ever known.

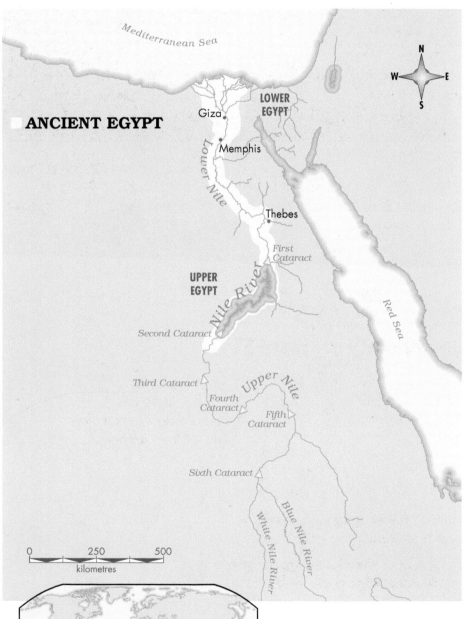

THE NILE RIVER

Every year, the Nile River floods. Nutrients and moisture from the river create a very fertile band of land on each side of the river. This area is called the Nile flood plain. The Egyptians called the dark, fertile soil around the Nile, *kemet*, or "black land." They called the dry land that surrounded it *deshret*, or "red land." It was along the fertile shores of the Nile that the wandering tribes of the desert first settled, becoming a civilization that would last for more than 3000 years.

The Nile is the longest river in the world and passes through very arid, or dry, land. It has many **tributaries**—streams and rivers that flow into it. Two of the Nile's major tributaries are the White Nile and the Blue Nile. The section made up of these two tributaries is called the **Upper Nile** because the land there is higher than that of the **Lower Nile**. The Nile crosses many **cataracts**, or waterfalls, on its way north. The first cataract separates the Upper and Lower Nile. In ancient times, the first cataract also separated Upper and Lower Egypt.

The top section of the Nile River, which flows into the Mediterranean Sea, is called the Lower Nile. The bottom section of the Nile River is called the Upper Nile because the land surrounding it is higher than that of the Lower Nile.

Egypt experiences extreme temperature changes between night and day, as well as between summer and winter. Temperatures are hot during summer days, averaging 40°C, and can drop to near freezing during winter nights. Despite these extremes, the Nile continues to provide nourishment to the land and the people, who have depended on it for thousands of years.

DIRECTION AND LOCATION

The Nile River flows north through eastern Africa. To understand direction and location, the **cardinal points**, or four major points of the compass, are used. These points are north (N), south (S), east (E) and west (W). North is located at the top of any map, south at the bottom, east to the right, and west to the left. Directions can also be used to give the location of one place compared to another. For example, the Red Sea is to the east of the Nile River. To give more accurate directions, **intermediate points,** which combine two directions, are given, for example, northeast (NE) and southwest (SW).

The water of the Nile River and the rich soil along its banks made it possible for the ancient Egyptians to farm and domesticate animals. They formed settlements and developed skills to improve their way of life.

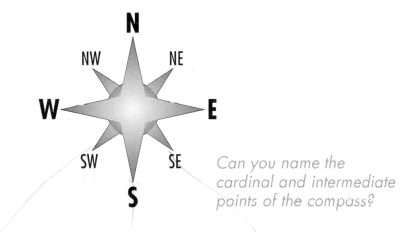

Can you name the cardinal and intermediate points of the compass?

SOMETHING TO DO

1. Explain how the flooding of the Nile helped the early Egyptians to grow their food. How did the Nile help Egyptian civilization to grow?

2. Find a map of modern-day Egypt in an atlas or on the Internet, and compare it to the map of ancient Egypt on page 16. Answer the questions below.

   a) How does the territory of Egypt differ on the two maps? How is it similar?

   b) Which country is located to the south of Egypt? Which country is located to the west? Name a country located southwest of Egypt.

   c) Which body of water is located to the north of Egypt? Which body of water is located to the east?

Egypt

3100–2650 BCE
Pre-dynastic Period
Upper and Lower Egypt
are united by King Narmer.

2040–1640 BCE
Middle Kingdom
Pharaohs lose some of
their power to local governments.

1070–332 BCE
Late Dynastic Period
Pharaohs start to lose power.
Many peoples, including the Assyrians
of Mesopotamia, invade Egypt.

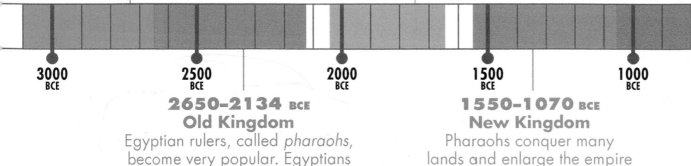

3000 BCE	2500 BCE	2000 BCE	1500 BCE	1000 BCE	500 BCE

2650–2134 BCE
Old Kingdom
Egyptian rulers, called *pharaohs*,
become very popular. Egyptians
build pyramids for the pharaohs.

1550–1070 BCE
New Kingdom
Pharaohs conquer many
lands and enlarge the empire
of ancient Egypt.

HISTORY

The history of Egypt is long and has been divided into different time periods. During the Pre-dynastic period, Egypt developed into two areas: Upper Egypt and Lower Egypt. Around 3100 BCE, there was a war between the two regions. Upper Egypt won the war, and its king, Narmer, brought the two regions together to form a united Egypt.

Although the pharaohs of ancient Egypt were usually men, four were women. This sculpture shows Hatshepsut, the first female pharaoh of Egypt, who ruled for 22 years during the New Kingdom period.

During the Old Kingdom, the rulers of Egypt, who were known as **pharaohs**, were very powerful. The people of Egypt considered them gods and constructed **pyramids** in which to keep them when they died. Pyramids were enormous tombs made from stone that were considered the pharaohs' home in the afterlife.

GOVERNMENT

An effective government takes care of its people and maintains order within a large kingdom. However, the primary role of the early Egyptian government was to support the pharaoh. To do this, Egypt was divided into regions called *nomes*, which were ruled by a *nomarche*. The nomarche reported to the pharaoh or his representative. Each nome had its own courts, treasury, and military.

As the government grew, more people were assigned to support the pharaoh. The **vizier** was second only to the pharaoh and helped him to manage the kingdom. Scribes recorded information for the pharaoh, managed business affairs, and prepared written documents, such as letters and wills.

SOCIAL STRUCTURE

The pharaoh was the supreme leader of Egyptian society. The nobles and military leaders held the highest positions in government. Priests performed religious duties, and scribes were respected for their ability to read and write. Craftspeople included weavers, sandal-makers, brick-makers, and carpenters. Most Egyptians were peasant farmers, while slaves were servants of the wealthy.

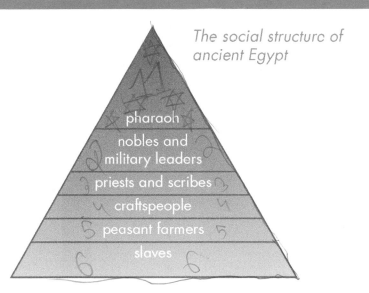

The social structure of ancient Egypt

pharaoh
nobles and military leaders
priests and scribes
craftspeople
peasant farmers
slaves

FAMILY LIFE

In ancient Egypt, an Egyptian boy entered manhood when he married, which usually took place in his late teens. Unlike the people of other ancient civilizations, Egyptians could marry for love and did not have to accept a marriage arranged by their parents. Since the family played an important role in ancient Egypt, having a baby was a very significant event.

The Egyptian woman's most important roles were that of wife and mother, and unlike Egyptian men, women did not hold jobs outside the home. During the New Kingdom, women gained the right to own property. They also had the right to make a will and divorce their husbands.

Common people lived in one- or two-room houses made of mud bricks. There was a staircase leading to the roof, where people would go to cool off during hot weather. Homes in the cities were built close together. They also had a staircase leading to the roof and sometimes contained a second or third floor.

In ancient Egypt, most clothing was made of white linen, which is a cloth made from the fibres of the flax plant. People went barefoot but wore sandals on special occasions. The ancient Egyptians ate bread, beans, onions and other vegetables, fruit, and fish from the Nile. They used clay jars, bowls, pots, and pans to prepare and store their food. Archaeologists have found these artifacts in Egyptian tombs.

Egypt

The ancient Egyptians were very superstitious. They wore amulets, or good-luck charms, such as the ankh, to protect them from evil. The ankh was the sign of life.

Important Egyptian gods and goddesses.

RELIGIOUS BELIEFS

Gods and Goddesses

Like the Mesopotamians, Egyptians worshipped many gods and goddesses. They believed that these gods controlled everything that happened in the world and that they could take the form of humans, animals, or a combination of both. The animal form of a god or goddess sometimes represented his or her personality. For example, a dog could represent loyalty, and a hawk or falcon could represent speed.

The ancient Egyptians believed that the pharaoh was able to communicate directly with the gods and goddesses. In fact, they believed that the pharaoh himself was a god—a descendant of the sun god, Ra. Priests represented the pharaoh in the many temples throughout Egypt and made offerings to the gods on his behalf. Most ordinary people worshipped at small local shrines, where they prayed to their favourite gods.

Afterlife and Mummification

The ancient Egyptians believed in the **afterlife**, that is, that there was life after death. To get into the afterlife, a dead person would have to be judged by Osiris, the god of the underworld, who would let the person in if he or she had led an honourable life. Priests performed spells and rituals to help the dead get into the afterlife.

An important step in the preparation for the afterlife was **mummification**, a technique used by the ancient Egyptians to preserve a dead body. Mummification developed over the centuries because the ancient Egyptians believed that a person's soul could return to his or her body if the body was properly preserved and kept in a tomb.

During mummification, the internal organs were removed from the body and stored in containers called **canopic jars**. The body was then dried using natron, a natural salt, and treated with resins and oils. The body

Ra
Sun God

Amun
Sun God who became linked to Ra

Anubis
God of Mummification

Osiris
God of Vegetation and Ruler of the Underworld

Isis
Wife of Osiris and Mistress of Magic

cavity was stuffed with linen, and the entire body, including the head, limbs, fingers, and toes, was wrapped in linen bandages. To protect the body from evil, charms, called **amulets**, were often placed within the mummy's bandages. A funeral mask, painted with the person's face, was placed over the mummy's head and shoulders. The mummy was then placed in a decorated coffin called a **sarcophagus**, which was often painted with the dead person's face. The sarcophagus was placed in a tomb along with food, furniture, and games. The ancient Egyptians believed that the person could use these items in the afterlife.

DID YOU KNOW?

Ground-up mummies were believed to heal and may have been used as medicine.

This Egyptian mummy is displayed beside its sarcophagus in a museum.

SOMETHING TO DO

Old Kingdom	Middle Kingdom	New Kingdom	Late Dynastic

1. Create a chart like the one above to show how the power of the pharaoh changed from the Old Kingdom to the Late Dynastic period.

2. Describe the terms *nome* and *nomarche*. What can we compare them to in Canada today?

3. a) Describe the role of the following people within Egyptian society: vizier, scribes, priests, and slaves.

b) Work in a small group to dramatize a scene that would show the role of each of these people in Egyptian society. Each person in your group should play one of these roles.

4. Create your own god or goddess. Draw him or her in animal form, and identify what he or she represents. Give your god or goddess a name.

5. Make a list of some of the prize possessions that you would want to have in the afterlife. Explain why you chose each item.

Egypt

*T*he ancient Egyptians had one of the longest lasting civilizations in history and gained great knowledge over the centuries. They used their knowledge to accomplish many important achievements in architecture, agriculture, science, and mathematics. Did you know that our number, monetary, and measurement systems originated in the number system first developed by the ancient Egyptians? The ancient Egyptians also discovered **papyrus**, one of the earliest forms of paper.

Beatrice

WRITING

The word **hieroglyphs**, or *medu netcher* in ancient Egyptian, means "words of the gods." Hieroglyphs are a form of communication that developed from picture writing and were used to decorate tombs and record information. Each picture represented a word or idea. Scribes used hieroglyphs to record stories, religious writings, history, and personal information. As the need to record information grew, so did the number of hieroglyphs. Eventually, the Egyptians developed an easier form of writing called *hieratic*, which looked like cursive writing.

Because the Egyptians needed to write down information about taxes and the activities of the pharaohs, they created the earliest form of paper, called *papyrus*. Papyrus was made of reeds that grew along the banks of the Nile. The Egyptians made papyrus by cutting the reeds into thin strips and pressing them together to make a sheet on which to write.

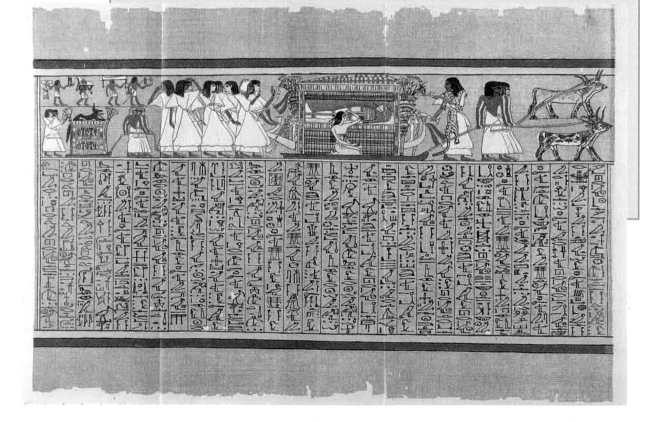

ARCHITECTURE AND CONSTRUCTION

The pyramids of Egypt are the oldest and largest stone buildings in the world. The ancient Egyptians built pyramids to keep the bodies of their dead pharaohs. A pharaoh's body was buried in a secret chamber inside or beneath the pyramid. These elaborate tombs were designed to house a pharaoh, his family, and his possessions for the afterlife.

The first Egyptian pyramids were step pyramids made of lime-stone. After 2600 BCE, larger, smooth-sided pyramids began to appear. Advanced technical knowledge, many workers, and a great supply of raw materials, such as stone, were needed to build the pyramids of Egypt.

Shifts of 10 000 workers from across Egypt spent three months at a time building the pyramids. The pyramids of Giza were built between 2600 and 2500 BCE. They took about 20 years to build and contain more than 2 million stone blocks. The pyramids of Giza are considered one of the seven wonders of the ancient world.

Egypt

SCIENCE AND MATHEMATICS

The ancient Egyptians gathered a great deal of information about the human body while preparing bodies for mummification. The information they gathered was used by both Greek and Arab scholars. Egyptian doctors developed skills in first aid, treating broken bones, performing minor surgery, and tending to some illnesses. Illnesses were treated with magic and medicine.

The Egyptian number system was based on the number 10, as is the number system that we use today. The Egyptians could calculate the area of two-dimensional figures and understood simple geometry. They used mathematics to calculate taxes and maintain property lines that were washed away during the flooding of the Nile. Much of what we know about Egyptian mathematics is based on the *Rhind Papyrus*, which is believed to be an early mathematics textbook.

The Egyptians measured the year according to the flood cycle of the Nile River and the stars that they observed in the sky. They developed a calendar that, like our own, was based on a year with 365 days. Their year, like ours, was divided into 12 months, and each month was made up of 30 days. Five days were left for religious celebrations.

EGYPTIAN NUMBER SYMBOLS

|	1
∩	10
℮	100
⚘	1 000
		10 000
𓅨	100 000
𓁨	1 000 000

AGRICULTURE

Rich soil, a favourable climate, and annual flooding provided a fertile strip of land along each side of the Nile River. Early settlers to the area grew wheat and barley to make bread and beer, as well as flax to produce linen. They raised cattle to work the land and to provide meat. As settlements grew and the number of crops increased, more land was needed to feed the population. Irrigation canals and dikes were used to move water during flooding and for the irrigation of dry land. During the New Kingdom, the Egyptians developed the **shaduf**. They used this device to raise water from the Nile or to move water from irrigation ditches to fields.

PERSONAL GROOMING

Personal grooming was important in the daily lives of ancient Egyptians. They were among the first people to use cosmetics, such as tooth powders, soaps, lipsticks, eye paint, wigs, and moisture cream. Both men and women in ancient Egypt used make-up and perfume. This ancient artifact shows women putting on perfume.

SOMETHING TO DO

1. Complete a chart like the one shown below to compare the pyramids of Egypt with the ziggurats of Mesopotamia.

	Ziggurats of Mesopotamia	Pyramids of Egypt
Use		
Materials Used		
Appearance		

2. Examine the picture of the shaduf on page 24, and explain how it helped the early Egyptians to irrigate their crops.

3. How have the achievements of the ancient Egyptians contributed to our world? Which achievement do you think is the most important? Why?

4. Write a message using your own hieroglyphs. Include a key with your message that shows the word or idea that each picture symbol represents. Exchange your message with a partner, and have him or her decode it using the key.

5. Create your own mathematical problem using the Egyptian numerals shown on page 24. Exchange your math problem with a partner, and have him or her calculate the answer.

Marcus was excited that his class was going to study Nubia. He knew that Nubia was a region of ancient Africa that stretched along the Nile River south of ancient Egypt. He had heard about the powerful Kush civilization of Nubia, which had ruled Egypt from about 750 to 670 BCE. Marcus went to the library to find out more about this ancient land. However, he was disappointed to find little information on the topic. Mr. Anderson, his teacher, explained that many of Nubia's archaeological treasures were destroyed, and that, until recently, few historians studied or were interested in this ancient region. These are some reasons why we know little about its civilizations. Ongoing excavations in the area may uncover more information about the people of this ancient land.

Today the region of Nubia is part of southern Egypt and the country of Sudan.

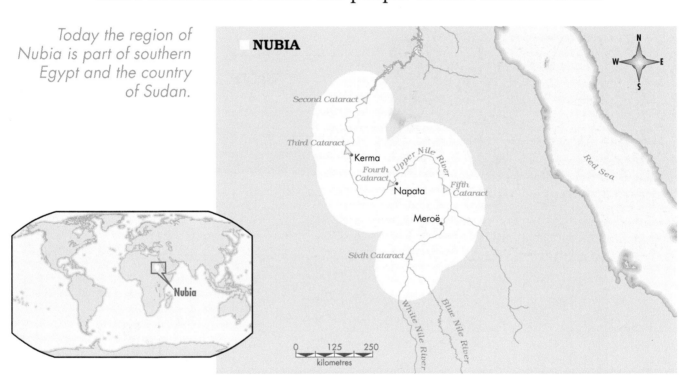

THE UPPER NILE

The villages and cities of Nubia developed along the Upper Nile. Cataracts, islands, swift currents, and shallow water make this section of the river very different from the Nile that flows through Egypt. In general, the flood plain along the Upper Nile is very narrow, which means that there is less fertile land for farming.

Unfortunately, we do not know very much about how people lived in ancient Nubia. Many artifacts were damaged or destroyed by early archaeologists and robbers and during the building of modern structures. In 1961, the **Aswan Dam** was built near the first cataract to provide Egypt and the area of ancient Nubia with water all year round. The dam flooded an area that contained many Nubian artifacts. Different countries sent archaeologists and engineers to help uncover Nubian artifacts and move large temples. However, since there was not enough time for a proper excavation, many artifacts were lost or destroyed.

Natural Environment

CLIMATE

Today Nubia is a hot, dry region. When people first started to settle in this area thousands of years ago, there was more rainfall. This made it possible for grasses and some trees to grow. People settled in the area and domesticated animals. They began to form villages along the Nile and its tributaries, where land was fertile and could support crops. Ancient rock drawings show that many wild and domesticated animals lived in the region.

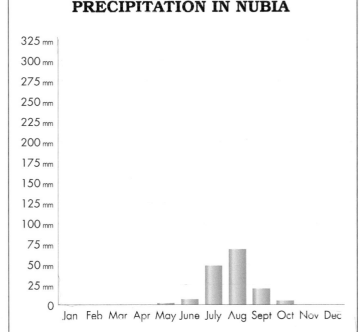

Artifacts, such as this ancient Nubian rock drawing, tell us about the types of animals that lived in the region. Which animal might this drawing represent?

The Upper Nile, which runs through ancient Nubia, is very different from the Lower Nile, which runs through ancient Egypt. How is it different?

PRECIPITATION IN NUBIA

This bar graph shows precipitation in the region of Nubia today. The graph shows how many millimetres of precipitation this area receives, on average, for every month of the year. **Precipitation** *is all the moisture that falls from the sky. Can you name three forms of precipitation?*

SOMETHING TO DO

1. Why have so few Nubian artifacts been found?

2. Draw how an ancient Nubian rock drawing might look, showing the wild and domesticated animals in that area.

3. Look at the graph showing precipitation in Nubia.

   a) How much rain does the region of Nubia receive on average in the month of January? Approximately how much does it receive in the month of August?

   b) Does the area of ancient Nubia receive a lot of rain? Explain your answer.

   c) How would the amount of rainfall in this area affect people's food supply?

Nubia

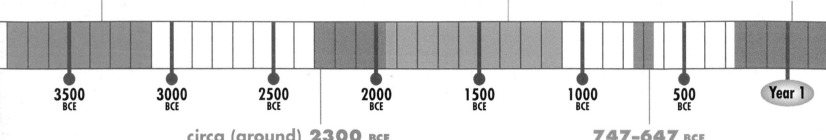

3800–3100 BCE
Ta-Seti Kingdom
Ta-Seti kingdom develops in Nubia around the second cataract of the Nile.

1950–1100 BCE
Egyptian Rule
Egypt rules Nubia and establishes temples, forts, and trade centres in the area.

270 BCE–250 CE
Kushites in Meroë
Meroë becomes the capital city o Kush. Kushite culture prospers.

3500 BCE — 3000 BCE — 2500 BCE — 2000 BCE — 1500 BCE — 1000 BCE — 500 BCE — Year 1

circa (around) 2300 BCE
Early Kush Civilization
Kush civilization begins to develop in southern Nubia. Kushite kings rule Nubia from the city of Kerma.

747–647 BCE
Kush Rule over Egypt
Kushite King Kashta conquers Egypt in 747. Napata is the capital city of Kush.

DID YOU KNOW?

On a recent expedition to Nubia, archaeologists of the Royal Ontario Museum, in Toronto, discovered hand axes, a stone tool workshop, and a shelter that could be 70 000 years old.

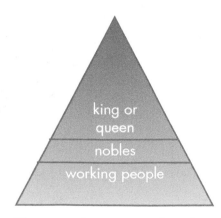

king or queen
nobles
working people

The social structure of Nubia

HISTORY

Much of what we know about Nubian civilizations comes from the writings of other peoples such as the Egyptians, Greeks, and Romans. These peoples, as well as early archaeologists, did not always describe these civilizations accurately. Modern archaeologists have tried to find more accurate information about Nubian cultures.

Evidence shows that people have lived in Nubia for thousands of years. Some people believe that the **Ta-Seti** kingdom is the oldest in history. The people of this community raised cattle; grew wheat; and traded gold, copper, special woods, animal skins, and ivory.

The Kush civilization had its own culture, government, and economy. Kushites were skilled metal workers and used a wheel to make high-quality pottery. Between 270 BCE and 250 CE, the Kushites produced iron and traded heavily with the peoples of ancient Egypt, India, Greece, and Rome. They also developed their own writing system and built great temples, palaces, and shrines in the city of Meroë.

GOVERNMENT AND SOCIAL STRUCTURE

Historians do not know very much about the government and social structure of Nubian civilizations because they still have not uncovered enough artifacts or written records. In Kush, there appears to have been a ruling class of nobles. There was also a working class of people who were farmers or labourers. Only a few people, who were often related to one another, controlled government and the **economy**. The economy consists of the wealth and resources of a community.

Between 270 BCE and 250 CE, both kings and queens ruled equally in Nubia. Both kings and queens led armies into battle. The queen, or **kandake,** raised and led armies, made decisions about the economy, and dealt with foreign lands. The mother of a king, or the queen mother, had the power to decide who would be the next king or queen and could remove a ruler who was not doing his or her job.

RELIGIOUS BELIEFS

The information that we have on Nubia's religious beliefs and practices comes mainly from Egyptian records and pictures that are carved on the walls of religious temples.

Nubia's early religious beliefs were based in part on those of Egypt. The people of Nubia became familiar with the gods and religious practices of Egypt through trade with the Egyptians. They later adopted these beliefs when Egypt ruled the region. In northern Nubia, Egyptian gods and goddesses became very important, the most important ones being Amun, Isis, and Osiris. As time passed, others became more important, including the Nubian gods Apedemak, the god of war; Dedun, the god of the four directions; and Dedwen, the god of incense. Incense is a substance that smells sweet when burned. It was one of the products that the Nubians traded for other goods.

Afterlife

Burial grounds have provided much of the information that we have about the Nubian people. The objects found buried in them show that the Nubian people believed in life after death. The dead of the Ta-Seti kingdom were laid beneath small mounds of earth along with different objects to use in the afterlife. These objects included elegant pottery, mirrors, stone palettes for grinding eye make-up, food jars, copper tools, and linen clothing.

The kings and queens of Kerma were buried in a central room of a **tumulus tomb**, which was a large mound of earth and stone used as a grave. Artifacts and hundreds of servants, who were killed to serve their masters in the afterlife, were placed along the hallway leading into the burial room. Thousands of cattle were killed and their skulls placed around the outside of the tomb. The cemetery at Kerma contained over 30 000 tumulus tombs, many of which were surrounded by thousands of black and white pebbles.

In the city of Napata, the Nubian people buried their kings and queens in pyramids along with their personal belongings. Like the Egyptians, they mummified their dead and kept their organs in canopic jars.

This artifact, showing a Nubian, was painted around 1160 BCE.

This picture of Apedemak, the Nubian god of war, was carved on the wall of a temple.

SOMETHING TO DO

1. a) How did the ancient Egyptians influence the religious beliefs of the Nubians?

   b) How were the religious beliefs of the Nubians different from those of the ancient Egyptians? Make a chart showing the similarities and differences.

2. Describe the duties of a Nubian queen and a queen mother. What might the duties of these women tell us about the role of women in Nubian society?

3. Pictures that are carved on the walls of religious temples have provided archaeologists with information on the religious beliefs and practices of ancient Nubia. Create one of these pictures on a slab of clay or Plasticine to illustrate something about the Nubian religion.

Nubia

The Kush civilization developed its own written language. However, scholars have not yet been able to understand it. We will find out more about Nubian civilizations and their achievements as archaeologists decode this written language and dig up more artifacts in the area. We do know that Nubia was an important trading centre of the ancient world and that the people of Nubia built pyramids. They were also skilled metal workers who used their tools to improve their land and produce more food.

WRITING

Early in their history, the Nubians used some of the Egyptian hieroglyphs to communicate and record information. Around 180 BCE, the Kushites developed their own written language. Historians call this language **Meroitic** because it was developed by the Kushites during the time that Meroë was their capital city. It uses word dividers to separate words and is read from right to left. Archaeologists have not been able to translate Meroitic writing, but they know the sounds that the symbols represent.

a		m		k	
e		n		q	
i		ne		t	
o		r		te	
y		l		to	
w		h		d	
b		s		word divider	
p		se			

TRADE

Nubia was a trading centre in the ancient world. Nubians traded goods with people who lived in central Africa as well as with the peoples of ancient Egypt, India, Greece, and Rome. Nubia's trade routes extended north, south, east, and west. Traders travelled in groups called **caravans**, using camels to transport their goods east to the Red Sea. Here they shipped them to India, the Arabian Peninsula, and the lands around the Mediterranean Sea.

The people of ancient Nubia traded gold, ivory, cattle, incense, animal skins, smelted iron, tools, weapons, and ebony (a dark heavy wood). They traded these items for cotton, grain, copper, and oil. Nubian traders used the **barter system**. This means that they traded items for other items and did not use money as we know it today. Traders had to negotiate or bargain for goods based on what they thought an item was worth. For example, an ivory tusk might be worth three barrels of oil or three canopic jars.

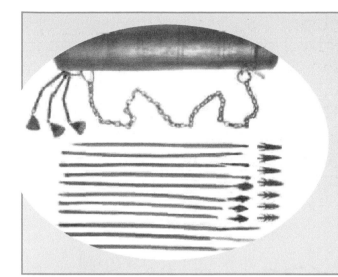

METALWORK

The people of Nubia were skilled metal workers. The Kush civilization of Nubia discovered iron and used it to make tools and weapons. They **smelted**, or heated, iron ore, which is the rock in which iron is found. They heated the rock in furnaces, using the trees in the area as fuel. Metal workers then used the iron that melted out of the rock to make tools and weapons, which they used and traded. Iron tools such as the hoe allowed Nubian farmers to improve their farmland. This made it possible for them to grow better crops.

ARCHITECTURE

The pyramids of Nubia were smaller than those of Egypt, but there were actually more pyramids in Nubia than in Egypt. The sides of Nubian pyramids were much steeper, sloping at approximately a 70-degree, rather than 51-degree, angle. Archaeologists believe that having sides this steep required a unique building technique.

Like the Egyptian pyramids, those in Nubia were made of stone. Although there were no rooms in these pyramids, a small temple was built on the outside, attached to the wall that faced east. People used these temples to make offerings of food to the dead. The Nubians buried their kings and queens under the pyramids in underground tombs.

SOMETHING TO DO

1. a) Why is it important that archaeologists understand Meroitic writing?

   b) Look at the English letters that the writing symbols represent, and use the symbols to write a sentence in Meroitic. Don't forget that Meroitic is written from right to left, and make sure to use the word dividers. Exchange your sentence with a partner, and have him or her translate your sentence into English.

2. Why was Nubia considered a trading centre of the ancient world?

3. Use books, CD-ROMs, and the Internet to research how iron is smelted in Canada today. How is it similar to the way it was done by the Kushites in ancient Nubia? How is it different?

4. Complete a graph like the one below to compare the pyramids of Nubia with those of Egypt.

	Pyramids of Egypt	Pyramids of Nubia
Use		
Materials Used		
Appearance		

O
nce there was nothing but a great, dark, deep sea. The sea wished to be more than it was, so it produced a single golden egg. After nine months, the time for a human or cow to be born, Parjapati broke out of the shell. Parjapati rested on the shell for a year, spending all that time thinking. After this time passed, Parjapati spoke, and these words became the earth, sky, and seasons. As time passed, loneliness set in. Parjapati divided to form two beings—a husband and wife. Together they created the first gods, the elements, time, and humans. Agni, the first born, became the god of fire. The light from Agni's fire was used to create daylight.

(Indian story describing how the world was created)

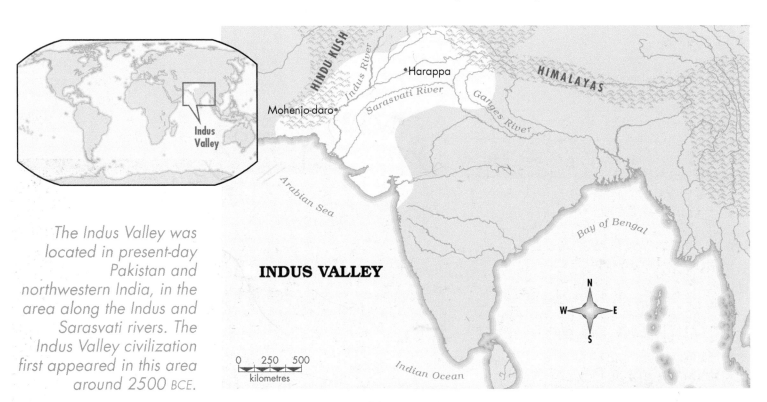

The Indus Valley was located in present-day Pakistan and northwestern India, in the area along the Indus and Sarasvati rivers. The Indus Valley civilization first appeared in this area around 2500 BCE.

THE INDUS AND SARASVATI RIVERS

In 1926, archaeologists discovered the remains of a great civilization that first appeared around 2500 BCE along the Indus River. This civilization is called the **Indus Valley civilization**. The people of this civilization lived in present-day Pakistan and northwestern India. Around 1500 BCE, the Indus Valley civilization was invaded by new settlers who came into the region from the northwest. These new settlers called themselves **Aryans**.

The area along the Indus River has always been a desirable place in which to live because of its warm weather and fertile land. The land in the area was made fertile by the flooding of the Indus and Sarasvati rivers. Early settlers in the area began to use the water of these rivers to irrigate their farms, and they created large, permanent settlements.

Rivers can flow in many directions. The course, or path, of a river can change over time. A river can even dry up and disappear. The Indus Valley and Aryan civilizations settled along the Indus and Sarasvati rivers. Through the centuries, these rivers changed a great deal. A drier climate caused the Sarasvati River to disappear. Some of the tributaries of the Indus River also vanished. This caused many people to move south and settle near other sources of water, such as the Ganges River.

CLIMATE

Around 3500 BCE, the climate of India and Pakistan was warmer and wetter than it is today. The grasses and trees that grew in the area provided food for many different types of animals, such as rhinoceroses, elephants, and water buffaloes.

During the year, seasonal **monsoons** occur in this part of the world. Monsoons are strong winds that change direction with the season. In the summer, the winds blow from the southwest, bringing warm, moist air from the Indian Ocean and causing the rainy season. In the winter, the winds blow from the northeast, bringing cool, dry air into the region.

DID YOU KNOW?

Scientists have drilled holes along the ancient Sarasvati riverbed and found water that is 3000 to 4000 years old.

The people who lived in the Indus Valley grew cotton. They may have been the first people to weave cotton into cloth. The photograph below shows the style of cotton clothing worn by the people of the Indus Valley civilization.

SOMETHING TO DO

1. a) Why did people want to settle in the area along the Indus River?

   b) Pretend that you are a new settler who has travelled to the Indus Valley from the north. Describe your new home in a short letter to a friend. Make sure to describe both the land and the climate.

2. How did the climate of ancient India and Pakistan change over time? How did this climate change affect the Indus and Sarasvati rivers and the people who lived near them?

3. Draw the Indus, Sarasvati, and Ganges rivers on an outline map of ancient India. Add arrows showing the direction of the winter and summer monsoons. Label the arrows.

India

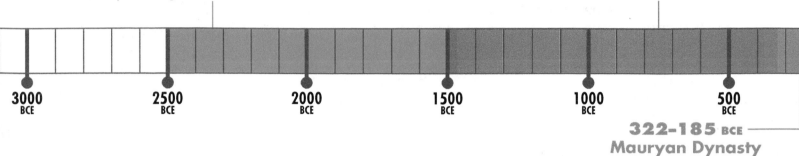

2500–1500 BCE
Indus Valley Civilization
Indus Valley civilization
develops along the Indus River.

circa (around) 1500 BCE
Arrival of Aryans
Aryans invade the Indus Valley region
from the northwest and settle in the area.

| 3000 BCE | 2500 BCE | 2000 BCE | 1500 BCE | 1000 BCE | 500 BCE |

322–185 BCE
Mauryan Dynasty
Mauryan dynasty creates an empire
by uniting all of the states in northern India

HISTORY

The earliest civilization of ancient India was the Indus Valley civilization. The two most important cities of this civilization were Mohenjo-daro and Harappa. They were both located in present-day Pakistan.

The Aryans tended large herds of animals and travelled around the grasslands of Asia and Europe. Some historians believe that they conquered the people of the Indus Valley civilization. Others believe that the Aryans settled and farmed alongside the people of the Indus Valley, learning farming techniques from them.

In 322 BCE, the Mauryan dynasty of the Magadha state created an empire by uniting all of the *mahajanapadas*, or states, in the region. A **dynasty** is a series of rulers or leaders who come from the same family. When the Mauryan dynasty ended in 185 BCE, India separated into smaller states. Later, many different people invaded India, bringing their ideas and opening up trade in the region.

GOVERNMENT

The civilizations of ancient India had different types of governments. The Indus Valley civilization seems to have had a government that tried to serve the needs of the people rather than those of a king or ruler. Archaeologists believe this because they have not uncovered any government or royal buildings; they have only uncovered public buildings, such as common baths and religious temples.

The Aryans lived in community groups that were led by a chief. The chief was either elected by the people or born into his position. These groups grew in power and later formed the 16 *mahajanapadas*, or states. When the Mauryan dynasty joined the parts of northern India together, there was a centralized government, or one in which the power was concentrated in a single area.

Most public buildings of the Indus Valley civilization seem to have been built to improve the life of the people. Archaeologists uncovered this public bath in Mohenjo-daro.

Society and Culture

SOCIAL STRUCTURE

Little is known about the social structure of the Indus Valley civilization. However, the social structure of the Aryans has been the basis of Indian society for thousands of years. According to the Aryans, it was the law of nature for people to belong to certain classes, or **castes**. The priests, who were the most powerful members of society, performed religious services and rituals. Next in power were nobles and warriors, followed by traders, craftspeople, and farmers. Servants worked for the higher classes.

There was another class of people outside the four castes known as **untouchables**. They were the people who had jobs that were considered "unclean," for example, removing dead animals and sweeping the streets.

FAMILY LIFE

Archaeologists are still investigating the Indus Valley culture. They have discovered that children played with objects, such as whistles, carts, and toy monkeys, and that people enjoyed music and dancing.

More is known about the family life of the Aryans because it is similar to family life in India today. In Aryan society, the father was the head of the family and had control over the lives of all family members. He made all the decisions. Women ran the household and did not have many rights. Parents decided whom their children would marry, and weddings were considered very special events. The parents of a girl or young woman offered a dowry to the man who would marry their daughter. A dowry is a gift of money or property to a groom.

The social structure of ancient India

Music was very important in ancient India. Instruments like drums and horns appear on many artifacts, such as this painting of a wedding scene.

Society and Culture

The Hindu god Vishnu is considered to be the preserver of the universe.

RELIGIOUS BELIEFS

The people of ancient India were very religious. **Hinduism** and **Buddhism**, two religions that are practised by millions of people around the world today, started in ancient India.

The Aryans worshipped many gods and goddesses. Some of their main gods were Vishnu, the preserver of the universe; Shiva, the changer of the universe; and Parvati, the mother goddess. Although they worshipped many gods and goddesses, the Aryans believed that all gods, people, and things were part of one supreme spirit and that everyone had a place in nature's order. The Aryans also believed in reincarnation. Reincarnation is the belief that when a person dies, his or her soul is reborn into another body. The Aryans believed that if a person was good, he or she would be born into a higher social caste in his or her next life. The religious beliefs of the Aryans developed into the religion known today as *Hinduism*, which is still the major religion of India.

The caste system that grew out of Hinduism made life very difficult for many people. Those who were in the lower classes were poor and had few rights. Siddhartha Gauthama, an Indian prince who lived between 563 and 483 BCE, started a new religion called *Buddhism*. He gave up all his belongings and later became known as the *Buddha*, or the "Awakened One." He believed that all people were equal and that they should be kind to all living things.

This is a statue of the Buddha. Who was he and what did he believe?

SOMETHING TO DO

1. Work in a group of five in which each student plays the role of a person belonging to one of the castes of Aryan society (including the untouchables). Describe how the caste system affects your daily life.

2. In 1950, the caste system was outlawed in India. Why do you think this happened?

3. Little is known about the people of the Indus Valley. Create four questions that you would ask an archaeologist who is studying this civilization to find out more about this culture.

Archaeologists are still discovering and collecting information on the civilizations of ancient India as excavation continues along the Indus River. The people who built the cities of the Indus Valley civilization were skilled engineers and town planners. They were also very good farmers. The civilizations of ancient India contributed greatly to our knowledge of city planning, farming, mathematics, medicine, language, and education.

CITY PLANNING

City planning was one of the greatest achievements of the Indus Valley civilization. The people of the Indus Valley seem to be the first to have designed their towns before building them. Streets were laid out in straight lines and were often located by a river, which made trade and transportation easier.

Buildings were either one or two storeys high, and they were made of bricks that were all the same size. This shows that the people of the Indus Valley used a system of measurement.

Unlike sun-dried bricks, which were easily damaged by rain, the clay bricks used by the people of the Indus Valley were baked. This made them last much longer. Indus Valley homes had flat roofs and contained four to six rooms, including a kitchen and a private bathroom. Many were two storeys high and had a private well on the property.

Underground pipes brought fresh water to the city and carried out sewage.

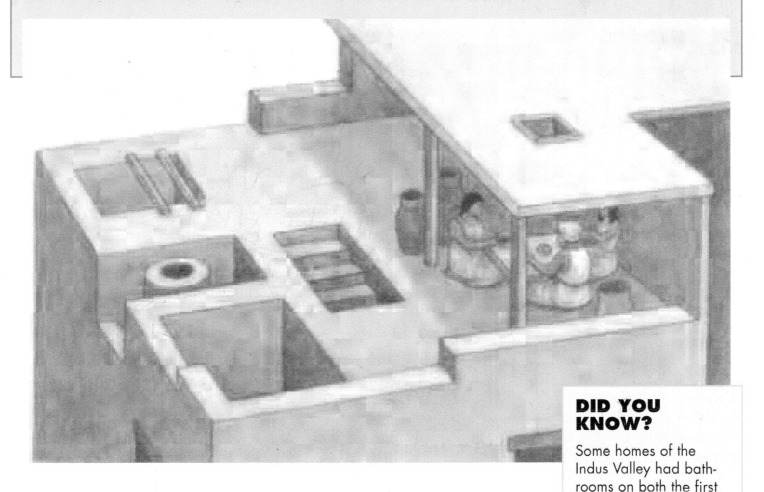

DID YOU KNOW?

Some homes of the Indus Valley had bathrooms on both the first and second floors.

India

FARMING AND IRRIGATION

The people of the Indus Valley were skilled farmers and grew barley, peas, melons, wheat, and dates. They also grew cotton and may have been the first people to make it into cloth. The people of this civilization also had many domesticated animals, including camels, goats, sheep, pigs, and buffaloes. Each town had a large **granary**, or building to store grain.

The civilizations of ancient India used many irrigation techniques to irrigate their crops. They dug tunnels, called **kareze**, into the ground until they found water. The kareze had a gradual slope that allowed water to flow out without pumps or water wheels. The earliest known **reservoir dam**, a water storage area for irrigation, was built in Saurashtra, India, in 150 BCE. The people of ancient India also used wells, dikes, and water wheels to irrigate their crops.

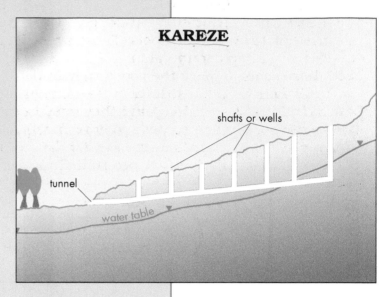

KAREZE

shafts or wells

tunnel

water table

SCIENCE AND MATHEMATICS

Kanada was an Indian philosopher who lived around 600 BCE. He believed that all objects could be broken down into extremely small particles called **parmanu**. These particles could not be felt by any part of the body or destroyed. Today these particles are known as atoms.

The decimal system, based on the number 10, that we use today is believed to have originated in the Indus Valley around 2000 BCE. The Indus Valley people used it to calculate the value, weight, and measure of products that they bought and sold.

In ancient India, doctors examined the environment of a patient as well as the patient's symptoms to determine the type of illness and treatment. Sushruta was a famous Indian surgeon who lived around 600 BCE. He was the first person to perform plastic surgery by fixing a patient's nose after it was cut off for a crime. Sushruta developed more than 120 surgical instruments in his lifetime. This illustration shows some of the surgical instruments that doctors used in ancient India.

WRITING AND LANGUAGE

The Indus Valley civilization developed a writing system that used pictures and symbols. These symbols appear on seals, or stamps, found along the Indus River. People used these seals to mark the goods they traded.

The Aryans brought with them the language of **Sanskrit**. This was the language they used in their religious writings. It was also used in government. Sanskrit has provided many words in the English language. The following English words developed from Sanskrit:

English	Sanskrit
mother	*matar*
brother	*bhratar*
orange	*naranj*

EDUCATION

The first university appeared in ancient India around 700 BCE. Students had to be at least 16 years old to attend, and they travelled from Greece, China, and Mesopotamia to learn from the **gurus**, or teachers. The university offered classes in 60 different subject areas and had as many as 10 500 students. Students studied subjects such as medicine, chemistry, metalwork, and the science of wealth. This photograph shows the ancient Indian city of Takshashila, where the first university was located.

SOMETHING TO DO

1. In small groups, create a model of an Indus Valley town or home using boxes, popsicle sticks, Plasticine, and/or other materials.

2. Why are the people of the Indus Valley considered skilled town planners?

3. Compare the houses in Canada to those of the Indus Valley civilization. Use a chart like the one below.

	Canadian House	Indus Valley House
Construction Materials		
Design		
Special Features		

6 China

T he god Pan Gu formed the earth and sky from the black egg in which he slept. Upon his death, his body became the many features we see on the earth and in the sky, but there were no people. The goddess Nu Wa decided to make them from yellow clay. She started to mould each person but found that it was too much work, and her strength was not great enough for the task. Nu Wa dipped a rope into the mud she was using to make people and allowed each drop to form an individual. Those she formed by her own hands became the wealthy nobles, and those falling from the rope became the peasants.

(Chinese story describing how people were created)

Since ancient times, the Chinese have been isolated from the rest of the world by mountains, deserts, and oceans. These physical barriers protected China from invaders, but they also made communication with other peoples difficult.

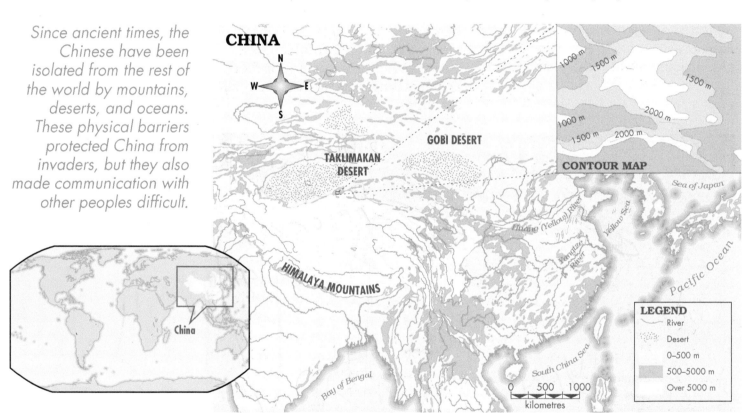

ELEVATION

Maps can be used to help understand how China's physical features have protected it over the centuries and influenced where people settled. Maps showing the physical features of an area use both colours and symbols. Colours show **elevation**, which is the height of the land above sea level. Symbols represent features such as deserts or rivers.

The height of the land can also be shown by **contour lines**.

Contour lines join points on the land of the same height. The height of each line can be written on the line or given in the legend. The difference in height between one line and another is called the **contour interval**.

LAND AND CLIMATE

Since most of China is made up of mountains or desert, only 15 per cent of its land is suitable for farming. The climate of northern China is very different from the climate in the south. In the north, winters are cold and summers are hot and somewhat dry. In the south, there is warm, moist weather all year round. The ancient Chinese grew millet, a type of grain, in the north and rice in the south. They also grew oranges, lemons, soybeans, peanuts, and sesame seeds.

THE YELLOW AND YANGTZE RIVERS

Chinese civilization developed along two rivers: the Huang He, which is also known as the **Yellow River**, and the Chang Jiang He, also known as the **Yangtze River**.

The Yangtze River is the longest river in China. It ends in a large **delta**. A delta is a fan-shaped deposit of **silt**, or tiny particles of earth, at the end of a river. The Chinese grow rice in this delta.

The Yellow River is named for the colour of the silt that it carries to the ocean. The nutrients of this silt make the banks of the Yellow River very fertile and good for farming. It is along the flood plains of the Yellow River that Chinese civilization began. There the nomadic tribes from the north began to grow crops and domesticate oxen, water buffaloes, and sheep, which they used for food and clothing and in their farming activities.

Millet

The Chinese have grown rice along the Yangtze River for thousands of years. What other foods did they grow?

SOMETHING TO DO

1. Look at the map of China on page 40. Refer to the legend to answer the following questions about the height of the land.

   a) What is the approximate height of the highest area in China? What is the name of these mountains?

   b) The Taklimakan Desert is located approximately how many metres above sea level?

   c) What is the approximate height of the land where the Yellow River empties into the Yellow Sea?

2. Look at the contour map of China on page 40. What is the contour interval? Recreate the contour map using contour lines. Label the height of each line. You may wish to colour the different elevations.

3. How did China's physical features affect the development of Chinese civilization?

China

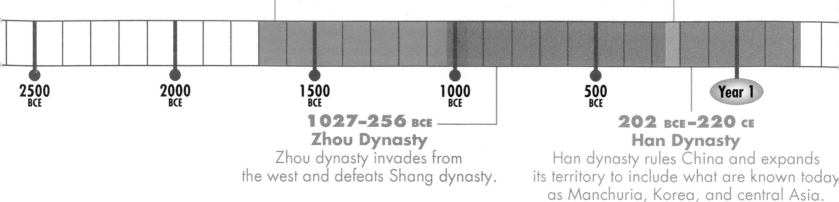

1700-1027 BCE
Shang Dynasty
Shang kings rule the area around the Yellow River.

256-202 BCE
Qin Dynasty
Qin dynasty rules China and expands its territory to includ what are known today as southern China and North Vietna

2500 BCE — 2000 BCE — 1500 BCE — 1000 BCE — 500 BCE — Year 1

1027-256 BCE
Zhou Dynasty
Zhou dynasty invades from the west and defeats Shang dynasty.

202 BCE-220 CE
Han Dynasty
Han dynasty rules China and expands its territory to include what are known today as Manchuria, Korea, and central Asia.

HISTORY

Around 3000 BCE, farming and fishing communities began to develop along the Yellow River. These settlements developed into a civilization ruled by dynasties. A dynasty is a series of kings or emperors who come from the same family. The first Chinese dynasty was the Shang dynasty. It was based on agriculture and the manufacturing of bronze and silk.

To defend themselves against nomadic tribes from the north, the people of the Zhou dynasty built walls along the northern edge of their territory. The first ruler of the Qin dynasty extended the walls that the Zhou had built to keep out invaders, creating the **Great Wall of China.** During the Han dynasty, the territory of ancient China was expanded, and the Chinese invented paper.

The Great Wall of China is the longest structure in the world. It is 2200 km long, 7.5 m high, and 4.5 m thick. Why was it built?

GOVERNMENT

The Zhou dynasty ruled by establishing a **feudal system**. The king gave out large portions of land to noble families who agreed to rule on the king's behalf. Nobles ruled these areas, collecting the rent from peasants who paid them for the right to farm the land.

This changed with the Qin dynasty, which centralized China's government by locating it in one city, Changan. It was important to create a powerful central government in China in order to protect the country from attack and to take on large building projects, such as the Great Wall. The Han dynasty created a large **civil service**, or group of government workers. These people had to go to government schools and pass examinations to take on different roles in the government.

The Han dynasty continued the system of central government established by the Qin dynasty.

SOCIAL STRUCTURE

The **emperor** or king was also the religious leader of Chinese society. People believed that heaven had given him the task of ruling China and that he was the link between heaven and earth. This was called the *Mandate of Heaven*.

Through the early dynasties, when feudalism was in place, the king and the nobles held most of the power and wealth of China. This changed during the Qin dynasty when all the power was centralized in the capital city and held by the emperor. During the Han dynasty, people of any class could get an important government job in the civil service, earning enough money to live a comfortable life.

Throughout all these dynasties, the peasant farmers, craftspeople, traders, and slaves served the nobles, performed military service, did manual labour, and paid all the taxes.

The first ruler of the Qin dynasty called himself Shi Huangdi, or "first emperor." He created a powerful central government in the capital city of Changan. Why was it important to have a centralized government in China?

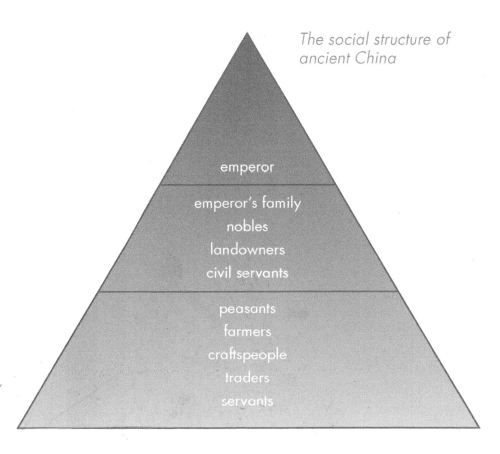

The social structure of ancient China

emperor

emperor's family
nobles
landowners
civil servants

peasants
farmers
craftspeople
traders
servants

FAMILY LIFE

For both rich and poor people, the family was the most important aspect of Chinese society. If one member of a family did something wrong, he or she would bring shame to the whole family. If he or she accomplished something, it would be considered an honour for the whole family.

In ancient China, families were usually large with grandparents, parents, and children living in the same household. The oldest male, usually the grandfather, was considered the head of the family. He decided whom his children would marry and what work his sons would do. Women were expected to respect their husbands and take care of the home and children. They also worked in the fields. Children were expected to obey their parents and grandparents.

For the Chinese, many traditional family roles and responsibilities and the idea of family honour continue to this day.

RELIGIOUS BELIEFS

Balance and Harmony

The Chinese believed that all parts of the universe were controlled by a force or energy called **qi** (pronounced *chee*). They believed that *qi* flowed through the earth and that it was important not to disturb it. They used the symbol of the **yin and yang** to represent the opposite forces of nature that are in harmony with each other. According to their beliefs, when people disturbed this harmony, they were punished with floods, earthquakes, and other natural disasters.

Ancestor Worship and the Afterlife

The early dynasties of Shang and Zhou believed in **ancestor worship**, a practice of making offerings of food and wine to relatives who had died. The ancient Chinese believed that when people died, their spirit lived in the afterlife and that they had magical powers.

An artist's interpretation showing family life in China. The Chinese wore silk clothing. This fine cloth was made from the thread produced by silk-worms, which fed on the leaves of mulberry trees. Silk from China was one of the most valuable products of the ancient world.

These spirits could bring either good or bad fortunc to an individual or a family. To keep their ancestors happy, people made offerings to them and held celebrations in their honour.

Oracles were used to communicate with ancestors. A question about the future would be carved in bone or on a turtle shell. The bone would be heated until cracks formed. An oracle would then "read" the pattern of cracks to answer the question.

Confucianism, Taoism, and Legalism

At the end of the Zhou dynasty, the Chinese followed three systems of belief. These philosophies continue to be important to the Chinese today.

Confucianism was based on the teachings of K'ung Fu-tzu, whose name means "Great Master Kung." He believed in an orderly society where everybody had a role, place, and responsibility. Chinese government and society were based on the principles of Confucianism.

The philosophy of **Taoism** is based on the teachings of Lao-tzu, who believed in living a simple life that was in harmony with nature. He believed that it was important to create a balance between the world of nature and the world of humans.

Legalism was a philosophy that encouraged people to obey authority. Supporters of this philosophy believed that to have an orderly society, the ruler had to have absolute, or total, power in order to control the people.

The Chinese have used the symbol of the yin and yang for thousands of years. It represents balance and harmony between the opposite forces of nature, for example, darkness and light, cold and heat, female and male.

The ancient Chinese made shrines inside and outside their homes to honour their ancestors. This photograph shows a modern shrine.

SOMETHING TO DO

1. Use a chart to show the differences among the systems of government of the Zhou, Qin, and Han dynasties.

2. Compare your family life with that in ancient China. List some of the differences and similarities.

3. a) In which philosophies did the ancient Chinese believe? Describe each one.

   b) Which of these philosophies would you like to live by? Why?

4. The yin and yang symbol represents the harmony and balance of the opposite forces of nature. Design your own symbol to represent harmony and balance. Make sure to use appropriate colours. Be prepared to present your symbol to the class.

China

Ancient China was a very inventive civilization. The ancient Chinese invented silk, paper, and the compass. Many Chinese innovations occurred in the last 200 years of the Han dynasty, which extended into the Common Era. These advancements include the seismograph (an instrument that measures earthquakes), fireworks, and the wheelbarrow.

SILK

Silk has been used as a natural thread in China for thousands of years. It is made from the cocoons of silkworms that live on mulberry leaves. The cocoon is spun by the silkworm to protect itself as it changes from a caterpillar into a moth. Cocoons are unwound and spun into thread, which is later woven into cloth. The cloth can then be dyed different colours and decorated with patterns or figures. Silk is light in weight and comfortable to wear. It is both beautiful and practical. The high demand for silk in ancient Greece and Rome led to the creation of a very long trading route called the **Silk Road**. It was 6400 km long, stretching west through central Asia to the Mediterranean Sea.

WRITING AND PAPER

Chinese characters are the oldest form of writing in use today. They first appeared as picture symbols on oracle bones during the Shang dynasty. As many as 5000 characters were used during the Shang dynasty. Since then, the Chinese have developed thousands of additional characters. **Calligraphy**, or fine writing, which is closely related to painting, was considered an art form in ancient China and still is in present-day China. The Chinese believed that the strength, balance, and flow of the writing strokes showed the writer's character.

Paper, as we know it, was invented in China during the Han dynasty. The first paper was made of hemp, rags, bark, and old fishing nets, which were pulped, or smashed together in water, to loosen the fibres. These fibres, or thread-like pieces of material, were gathered on a silkscreen to allow the water to drain. The pulp was then rolled into thin sheets.

COMPASS

A compass is an instrument that shows direction. Compasses were used by the ancient Chinese for religious purposes or to tell the future. Later the Chinese used the compass for navigational purposes.

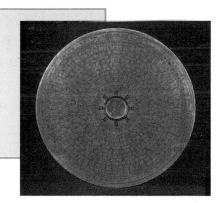

SCIENCE AND MATHEMATICS

The oldest medical texts in China were written between 300 and 200 BCE. They described the major organs of the body by size, weight, and colour and contained ideas about the circulation of blood. The Chinese believed in holistic medicine, which treats a person's mind and spirit as well as his or her body. The *qi*, a person's life force or energy, was treated through the use of herbs and **acupuncture**. Acupuncture is a way to treat disease and pain by inserting needles into a patient's body at special points. The Chinese believe that acupuncture stimulates the *qi* and restores balance to the unhealthy body part. Today acupuncture is a popular method of medical treatment in Canada and other parts of the western world.

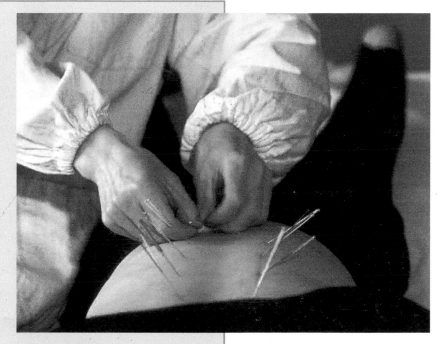

The ancient Chinese were some of the most advanced astronomers of the ancient world. Astronomy was so important to the Chinese that they built an observatory, a building used to view and study the night sky, in 1000 BCE.

The emperor was responsible for creating the calendar to show farmers when they had to plant and harvest crops. The ancient Chinese were the first people to establish the length of the year at 365 days.

SOMETHING TO DO

1. Which invention do you think is ancient China's most important contribution to the development of the modern world? Explain your answer.

2. Compare the medical knowledge of ancient China to that of another ancient civilization. Identify the similarities and differences.

3. What is acupuncture? Would you use this type of medical treatment to cure your ailments? Why or why not?

7 Greece

Have you ever read the story "The Tortoise and the Hare"? Have you heard of the mythical creatures Pegasus, Medusa, or the Minotaur? They are all creations of the ancient Greeks. Ancient Greek fables and myths describing the adventures of fascinating characters have interested people for centuries. However, the influence of ancient Greece extends beyond its fables. The ideas of the philosophers, artists, and writers of ancient Greece have helped to shape our modern world. As well, it was in ancient Greece, one of the first civilizations of Europe, that **democracy**, or rule by the people, was born.

Ancient Greece developed beside the eastern Mediterranean Sea in the area of modern-day Greece and western Turkey. This civilization began to appear on the island of Crete around 2000 BCE.

LAND AND SEA

Unlike the civilizations of Mesopotamia, Egypt, India, and China, which depended on rivers, ancient Greece depended on the sea. This ancient civilization developed in the eastern Mediterranean on the mainland of modern Greece and on the tiny islands of the Aegean Sea. The territory of ancient Greece also included the western shores of modern-day Turkey. Greece is surrounded by sea. Its coastline is over 3200 km long. The **natural harbours**, or sheltered areas of the coastline, provided protection for boats. Boats sailed from these harbours to fish and to exchange products and ideas with other civilizations around the Mediterranean.

Greece is a rugged and mountainous land. Like the sea, the mountains had a great effect on the way Greek civilization developed. While the mountains protected Greece from invaders, they also isolated Greek settlements from one another. This led to the development of very independent Greek city-states, which often fought one another.

The hilly land was ideal for raising sheep and goats. There were few rivers, and only small pockets of land were fertile enough to farm. The ancient Greeks grew olives, figs, grapes, and barley for their personal use and for trade.

CLIMATE

Greece has a Mediterranean climate. Its summers are hot and dry, and its winters are mild. There is little rainfall and not very much water available for agriculture. There are few rivers, and most contain water only in the winter or after a storm. In the hot summer, most rivers are dry or contain very little water.

MAP GRIDS

On the map of ancient Greece, there is a grid. A **map grid** is a set of imaginary lines that uses letters and numbers to help people find places on a map. Numbers and letters are written along the edges of the grid to identify each square. The letter–number combination of each square makes it easy to locate places on the map. For example, Mount Olympus is located at D1.

Natural harbours along the coastline of Greece, like this one, provide protection for boats. In what ways did ancient Greece depend on the sea?

DID YOU KNOW?

Growing olives was a difficult and costly task because trees grew for 16 years before producing olives. Many people were needed to harvest and press the olives to make olive oil.

SOMETHING TO DO

1. Look at the map of Greece on page 48, and answer the questions below.

   a) In which square of the map grid is Athens located?

   b) Name the places located in the following squares of the map grid:
      - F6
      - D4
      - C4

2. Look at the map on page 48. Colour the territory of ancient Greece on an outline map. Label the Aegean Sea, Mount Olympus, Crete, Athens, and Sparta. Use the map grid as a guide.

3. Using a diagram or a chart, name three advantages and three disadvantages of living in ancient Greece. Consider both the climate and physical landscape.

Greece

2000–1450 BCE
Minoan Civilization
Greek civilization first appears
on the island of Crete.

800–480 BCE
Mediterranean City-States
Greeks establish settlements in
present-day Italy, Spain, France,
and northern Africa.

480–338 BCE
Athens and Sparta
Athens and Sparta become
the most powerful city-states.

| 2500 BCE | 2000 BCE | 1500 BCE | 1000 BCE | 500 BCE | Year |

1600–1100 BCE
Mycenaean Civilization
Powerful city-state of Mycenae
develops on mainland Greece.

334–27 BCE
Alexander the Great's Empire
Alexander the Great conquers many lands
and expands the Greek empire to include
India, Persia, and Egypt.

HISTORY

The first civilization of Greece was called the **Minoan** civilization after its legendary king, Minos. Crete was a centre of trade between the Minoan people and others, such as the Egyptians and the Mesopotamians. Minoans were skilled craftspeople, merchants, and shipbuilders.

The people of **Mycenae** farmed and manufactured and traded goods. They also attacked other city-states to rob them of their wealth. Mycenaeans spoke a language on which modern Greek is based.

Greek city-states developed very differently from one another, having their own government, army, money, and laws. Between 480 and 338 BCE, the two most powerful city-states emerged— **Athens** and **Sparta**. Athens was a great trading and artistic centre. Sparta was a city-state with a highly trained army.

The Greek city-states were defeated by Philip II of Macedonia. He and his son, Alexander the Great, created a powerful army that conquered many lands. Alexander's empire spread the Greek language and culture to many parts of the world.

GOVERNMENT

As Greek civilization developed, so did its governments. Many city-states were ruled by tyrants, cruel leaders who held absolute power over all the people. In Athens, the people rose up against ruling tyrants and created a democracy. Democracies allow the people of a community to have a say in government decisions.

All male Athenians, whether rich or poor, belonged to the **Assembly** and were allowed to

All male Athenians over the age of 18 belonged to the Assembly and were allowed to vote.

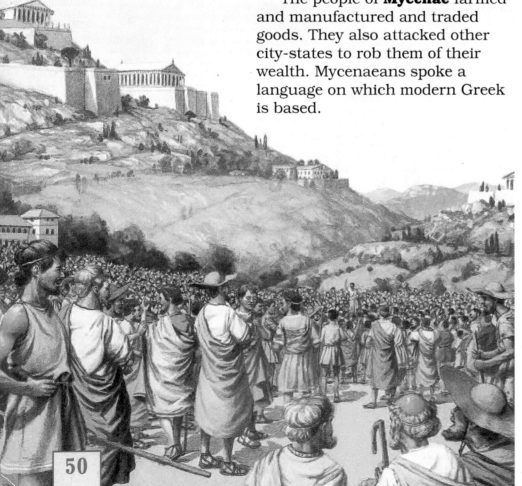

50

vote on many different matters, including how to maintain roads and when to hold festivals. They voted on these matters regularly, at open meetings, by raising their hands to agree or disagree with laws suggested by the **Council**. The Council was made up of 500 citizens who prepared laws for the Assembly to consider. The Athenians decided who would serve on the Council by drawing names. Members served on the Council for one year.

SOCIAL STRUCTURE

Athenian **citizens** were men who came from many backgrounds and had the freedom to work as farmers, craftspeople, and traders. Spartan citizens entered military service at the age of seven. They were trained to protect Sparta from attacks and uprisings from slaves. In both Athens and Sparta, the wives of citizens did not have the right to vote. People from other lands were allowed to work and had to serve in the military but were not allowed to vote. The Athenians treated slaves well, but the Spartans treated their slaves harshly.

FAMILY LIFE

In most of ancient Greece, boys went to school from the ages of 6 to 14. At school, they learned reading, writing, poetry, arithmetic, drawing, and painting. At the age of 14, they started their physical training at public gyms and by participating in sports. At the age of 18, boys started their military service, which lasted for two years. In Sparta, which was a military society, boys served in the army from ages 7 to 20. Greek men usually married around the age of 30.

In most of ancient Greece, girls did not attend school. They stayed home and learned reading, writing, arithmetic, and household chores from their mothers. They got married at an early age to mates chosen by their fathers. Women spent the day at home running the household and taking care of the children. In Sparta, girls were expected to participate in athletics to strengthen their bodies. It was believed that this would help them produce healthy children.

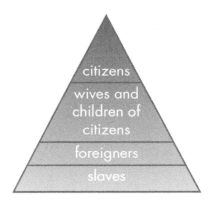

The social structure of ancient Greece

Women in ancient Greece wore linen dresses fastened at the shoulders with pins. They used olive oil to prepare their meals, which often included cheese and fish. Why is it not surprising that they ate these foods?

RELIGIOUS BELIEFS

The ancient Greeks used imaginative stories to explain life and creation. These stories, which are usually about the supernatural adventures of gods, heroes, and other creatures, are called **myths**.

The Myth of Athena and Arachne

Arachne was a famous weaver from the country of Lydia, a place known for its fine cloth. She boasted that her weaving abilities were as great as those of the gods. Athena, the goddess of wisdom and crafts, heard her arrogant words and decided to teach Arachne a lesson. She changed her own appearance, as most gods and goddesses could, to that of an old woman. As an old woman, Athena warned Arachne not to compare herself to the gods. Arachne did not listen, so Athena challenged her to a weaving contest.

Both produced magnificent tapestries, which are fabrics in which coloured threads are woven to form patterns or designs. Athena's showed the fate of humans that compared themselves to the gods, while Arachne's illustrated the loves of the gods.

Athena was so jealous of Arachne's beautiful work that she struck the woman and changed her into a spider. And that is why spiders weave webs.

DID YOU KNOW?

The scientific name for a spider is *arachnid*, which comes from the name Arachne.

Gods and Goddesses

The ancient Greeks worshipped many gods. Like the gods of Mesopotamia and Egypt, Greek gods were **anthropomorphic**, which means that they had human characteristics and experienced human feelings and events. The ancient Greeks believed their gods were all-powerful and controlled all aspects of the universe. Twelve gods—six male and six female—were worshipped more than any others. They lived on **Mount Olympus**, in northern Greece, and their leader was **Zeus**, god of the sky.

The ancient Greeks worshipped their gods and goddesses by building temples, creating statues, and celebrating festivals in their honour. Individuals offered animal sacrifices, fruits, or other gifts at shrines and temples to please the gods.

When people wanted answers to questions about the future, they often consulted an oracle, a person who was thought to communicate with the gods. These oracles were priests or priestesses who communicated with a particular god at a shrine or temple.

Hera · Poseidon · Artemis · Zeus · Hermes · Aphrodite · Hestia · Hephaestus · Athena · Demeter · Ares · Apollo

SOMETHING TO DO

1. a) What is the meaning of the word *democracy*?

   b) As a class, play the roles of the Assembly and the Council of Athenian democracy to vote on school issues.

2. a) What is a myth? Summarize the myth on page 52 in your own words.

   b) The ancient Greeks used myths to explain creation and natural occurrences. Write your own Greek myth to explain a natural occurrence. Use Greek gods as characters in your myth. Present your myth in the form of either a comic strip or an illustrated booklet.

3. Use a chart like the one below to compare the gods of ancient Greece, Mesopotamia, and Egypt. How are they similar? How are they different?

	Greece	Mesopotamia	Egypt
Principal Gods			
Characterisitics of Gods			
What Principal Gods Represent			

These are the most important Greek gods: Zeus, god of the sky and leader of the gods; Hera, goddess of marriage and childbirth; Poseidon, god of the sea and earthquakes; Demeter, goddess of the earth and crops; Hestia, goddess of the home; Athena, goddess of wisdom and crafts; Apollo, god of the sun and music; Artemis, goddess of hunting and the moon; Hermes, messenger of the gods; Aphrodite, goddess of love and beauty; Hephaestus, god of metalwork; and Ares, god of war.

Greece

The ancient Greeks questioned everything. They valued knowledge above all. It is hard to list all the accomplishments of this ancient civilization. They include a democratic system of government, competitive sports, the alphabet, certain styles of architecture, and new ideas in the areas of drama, literature, science, and mathematics.

THE ALPHABET

The ancient Greeks created the first **alphabet** that contained both consonants and vowels. This alphabet developed into the English alphabet that we use today.

ARCHITECTURE

The ancient Greeks built great temples to honour and worship a specific god or goddess. They designed their temples using mathematics to make sure that the size and shape were appealing. Buildings were balanced and well proportioned. Temples included a long hall with rows of columns on the outside supporting the roof.

This photograph shows the Parthenon. It was an ancient temple dedicated to the goddess Athena.

ART

Ancient Greek sculptors were famous for making statues of the human form. They created statues of gods, goddesses, and human beings. Sculptors made their statues beautiful by trying to achieve harmonious proportions, or attractive and balanced parts. Over the centuries, artists learned to make their works more lifelike and show human emotion. Most artists created their statues from stone; however, some artists also used bronze. The work of the ancient Greek sculptors influenced the artists of future European civilizations and is still studied by artists today.

LITERATURE

The poems the **Iliad** and the **Odyssey** are two of the greatest adventure stories in literature. It is believed that Homer wrote them between 800 and 700 BCE. The *Iliad* tells the story of the Trojan War and includes such famous characters as Helen of Troy and Achilles. The *Odyssey* is the story of Odysseus, a king who, during his travels, comes face to face with Cyclops, the one-eyed giant, and many other memorable characters.

Other famous literature from ancient Greece includes **Aesop's fables**, stories that we still read today. Many people are familiar with these short animal stories that have a moral message. They include "The Hare and the Tortoise," "The Boy Who Cried Wolf," and "The Ant and the Grasshopper" among many others. Most people believe that Aesop was a slave who wrote his stories around 600 BCE.

Drama is another form of literature for which the ancient Greeks are famous. The theatre was a favourite pastime for the ancient Greeks, who would sit for hours watching plays. Like modern plays, their plays had directors, actors, costumes, and scenery. A group of people, called a *chorus*, narrated the story by singing about it. The European civilizations that followed based their plays on those of ancient Greece. This photograph shows an illustration of an ancient Greek theatre.

Greece

THE OLYMPICS

The **Olympic Games** originated in ancient Greece. They were held every four years, between 776 and 396 BCE, to honour Zeus at his most famous shrine, in Olympia. The games lasted five days. Boys and men from all the Greek city-states participated in the Olympics. In fact, the ancient Greeks put their wars on hold during the games so that their athletes could compete against one another.

Ancient Olympic Games Program

Day 1		Sacrifices, oaths, and checking of athletes
Day 2	Morning	Horse and chariot races
	Afternoon	Pentathlon, a combination of five events: sprinting, long jump, wrestling, javelin throwing, and quoits (an activity in which a person throws a stone or metal ring at a peg)
Day 3	Morning	Religious ceremonies
	Afternoon	Boys' events
Day 4	Morning	Track events
	Afternoon	Wrestling, boxing, racing in armour
Day 5		Banquet and sacrifices

Socrates

PHILOSOPHY

Greek **philosophers**, or thinkers, discussed and debated ideas about science, law, human emotions, good, and evil. Their ideas influenced the philosophers of the world. Socrates (470 to 399 BCE) was a famous Greek philosopher who believed that each person had a soul that should strive for good. He also questioned whether the gods really existed. Plato (427 to 347 BCE) was another Greek philosopher who was a student of Socrates'. His main interest was politics, the study of government. He wrote *The Republic*, which was the first book ever written about politics. Aristotle (384 to 323 BCE) was a student of Plato's. He was interested in biology, the science of living organisms. Modern biology is based on his system of investigation.

SCIENCE AND MATHEMATICS

Many ancient Greek philosophers studied geometry, which is the mathematical study of lines, angles, and shapes. Pythagoras (582 to 500 BCE) was a mathematician who studied the pattern of numbers. He developed the Pythagorean theorem. Students study his theorem in math class today. Archimedes (287 to 212 BCE) studied the circle and worked on the value of *pi*. Pi is a value that stays the same and can be used to calculate different parts of a circle.

The ancient Greeks had a great knowledge of astronomy. They knew that Earth was round and that it revolved around the sun. At that time, most people believed that the sun, moon, and stars revolved around Earth.

By the fifth century BCE, Greeks started to develop medical treatments for all kinds of diseases. They studied Egyptian medical texts, learned more about herbs and ointments, and began studying symptoms, or signs, of specific illnesses. Hippocrates (460 to 367 BCE) is considered to be the father of medicine. He wrote about different illnesses and their treatment, as well as how a doctor should behave. Hippocrates believed that doctors should take an oath promising that they would treat their patients to the best of their abilities. This vow is called the **Hippocratic oath**.

> The Hippocratic Oath.
> I swear ... that according to my ability, I will keep this oath: ... to follow that system of treatment which I believe will help my patients, and to refrain from anything that is harmful to them. I will give no deadly drug if I am asked to do so, nor will I recommend any such thing....

SOMETHING TO DO

1. "The ancient Greeks have had a great influence on modern civilization." Do you agree with this statement? Explain your answer by providing examples.

2. Look at the Greek alphabet on page 54. How can you tell that it is an early form of the alphabet that we use in English today?

3. Look in books or on the Internet to find examples of Aesop's fables. Summarize your favourite fable. Why is it your favourite?

4. Compare the modern-day Olympics to those of ancient Greece. Identify similarities and differences.

5. Identify a contribution of the ancient Greeks in each of the following areas. Explain why each contribution is important.

   • Medicine

   • Philosophy

   • Mathematics

DID YOU KNOW?

Doctors today still take the Hippocratic oath when they graduate from medical school.

R omulus and Remus were the twin sons of the god Mars and Rhea Silvia, the daughter of a king. After Amulius killed Rhea's father and brothers, he took over the throne. Because he was worried that Rhea's children would take back the throne when they grew up, Amulius ordered that they be set adrift in a basket on the Tiber River. The twins were rescued from the river by a she-wolf who nursed them. Later they were found and raised by a shepherd. Romulus and Remus got revenge for what had happened to their family by taking back the throne and building a city where they had washed ashore. The two brothers fought during the construction of the city, and Remus was killed. Romulus named the city Rome.

(The legend of Romulus and Remus)

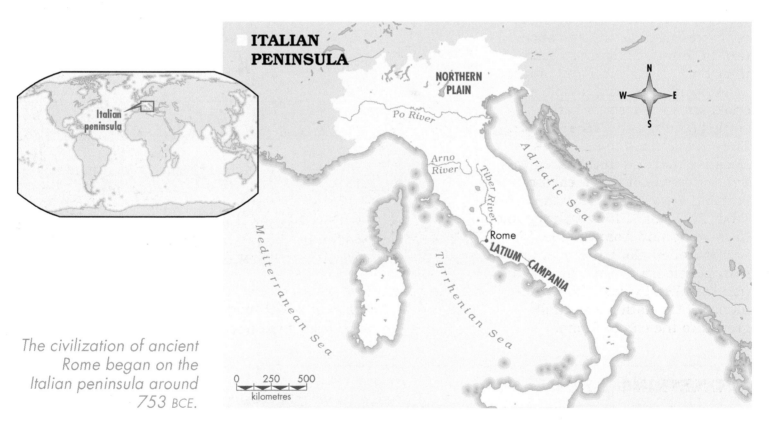

The civilization of ancient Rome began on the Italian peninsula around 753 BCE.

THE ITALIAN PENINSULA

On a map of the Mediterranean Sea, you will notice what looks like a boot kicking a rock. This is the **Italian peninsula**, the land of the ancient Romans. Although its coastline was quite long, there weren't many good harbours. However, its location in the middle of the Mediterranean Sea made it easy for the ancient Romans to travel by boat to other lands, such as Greece and northern Africa. The Po, Arno, and Tiber rivers were very important in the development of the Roman Empire. Travel, trade, and communications depended on these rivers and the sea.

Natural Environment

Like Greece, the land of the Italian peninsula is hilly and mountainous. This made transportation and communication difficult in ancient times. There were three main areas of fertile land on the Italian peninsula: the Northern Plain and the plains of Latium and Compagnia. Volcano eruptions on the Italian peninsula had made the soil of Latium and Campania very fertile. The volcanic ash that had been deposited on the land contained phosphates. Phosphates are often added to soil to help plants grow. The ancient Romans also mixed volcanic ash with water to make concrete. They used this important building material to make their homes and other buildings.

Around 1200 BCE, people who spoke an early form of Latin settled south of the **Tiber River**. They are referred to as Latins. Because the land in this area was flat and fertile, it was ideal for farming. Its location near the Tiber River made it easy for people to travel to and from the sea. The Latins traded along the river and with people from other lands who had travelled by sea. The settlements of the Latins eventually grew into the city of Rome.

CLIMATE

Much of the Italian peninsula has a Mediterranean climate. Like Greece, it experiences mild, rainy winters and hot, dry summers. The climate in the north is cooler, and rain is plentiful. The climate of the Italian peninsula is ideal for farming, and the ancient Romans grew olives, grapes, and wheat. These crops are still grown there today.

People have grown olives, grapes, and wheat on the Italian peninsula for more than 2000 years. What types of food could they have produced from these crops?

SOMETHING TO DO

1. How did the volcanic ash in the soil of the Italian peninsula help the Romans to grow their food and build their homes?

2. How was the natural environment of ancient Rome similar to that of ancient Greece? How was it different? Use a Venn diagram like the one shown here to list the differences and similarities.

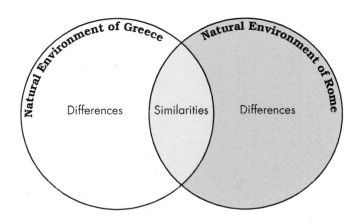

Natural Environment of Greece — Natural Environment of Rome

Differences — Similarities — Differences

Rome

circa (around) **753** BCE
Creation of Rome
The villages of the Latins along the Tiber River joined to form the city of Rome.

509–31 BCE
Roman Republic
Romans overthrow Etruscans and form the Roman Republic.

circa (around) **31** BCE
Beginning of the Roman Empire
The Roman Republic ends and the Roman Empire begins.

| 2000 BCE | 1500 BCE | 1000 BCE | 500 BCE | Year 1 | 500 CE |

601–509 BCE
Etruscan Rule
The powerful army of the Etruscans invades and conquers Rome.

49 BCE
Julius Caesar
Julius Caesar takes control of Rome.

*The civilization of Rome has both a legendary and historical beginning. A **legend** is a story from the past that people believed to be true. According to legend, Rome was founded in 753 BCE by the twin brothers Romulus and Remus. The twin babies were rescued from the Tiber River by a she-wolf.*

DID YOU KNOW?

In addition to fighting, Roman soldiers were trained to build forts and roads and act as police officers in the Roman provinces.

HISTORY

When the villages of the Latins formed the city of Rome, two other ancient civilizations lived on the Italian peninsula—the Greeks and the Etruscans. The Greeks established city-states on the southern Italian peninsula. The **Etruscans**, a wealthy and very skilled civilization, had established a number of city-states north of Rome.

After the Romans overthrew the Etruscans, they formed the Roman Republic. A **republic** is a form of democratic government in which the people hold the power and have the right to vote. During the Roman Republic, Rome developed a very powerful and efficient army. Troops were organized into **legions**, which were groups of 3000 to 5000 soldiers. Each legion was divided into groups that were given different roles and duties in battle. This made the army very effective. The Roman army conquered all the peoples of the Italian peninsula and of many other lands across Europe, Africa, and the eastern Mediterranean. The Romans called their conquered lands **provinces.**

Society and Culture

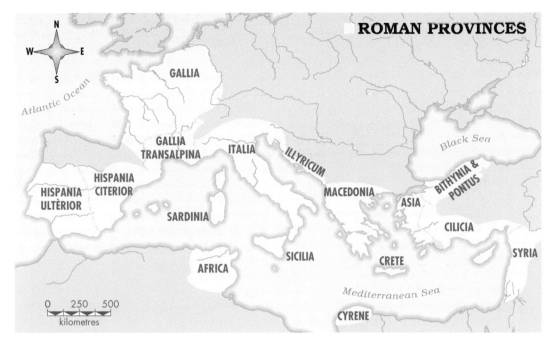

ROMAN PROVINCES

The civilization of ancient Rome began around 750 BCE and grew from a single city on the banks of the Tiber River to a huge and powerful empire that stretched across Europe and around the Mediterranean Sea.

GOVERNMENT

Ancient Rome experienced different types of governments. When the Etruscan kings ruled the Romans, the government was a **monarchy**. A monarchy is a form of government in which a king or queen rules the people. The ruler of a monarchy is born into his or her position of power.

During the Republic, male citizens of Rome had the right to vote and have a say in government decisions. In the early Republic, **patricians**, or wealthy landowners, formed the **Senate**, which was a group of men who governed Rome. The Senate's power increased so that common working people, called **plebeians**, had little say in government decisions. In 494 BCE, the plebeians demanded a greater say in government and were able to form their own assembly called the *Concilium Plebis*.

Roman army generals fought for control of the Republic. One such general, Julius Caesar, took control of the Senate and became **dictator** of Rome in 49 BCE. A dictator is a ruler who has absolute, or total, power over a people and its government.

In 31 BCE, Caesar's nephew, Octavian, became the first emperor of Rome. He was given the name Augustus, which meant "the highest one." This marked the end of the Roman Republic and the beginning of the Roman Empire. No longer a republic ruled by the people, Rome became a **dictatorship**. In a dictatorship, one person holds all the power.

Julius Caesar

Each Roman soldier carried a heavy load of tools, weapons, and a shield, as well as personal possessions.

Rome

SOCIAL STRUCTURE

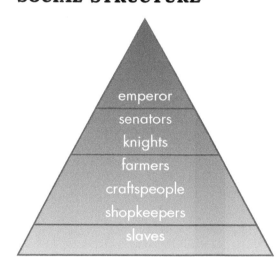

The social structure of ancient Rome

The most powerful person of the Roman Empire was the emperor. Patricians, the wealthy families of Rome, were either senators or knights. Farmers, shopkeepers, and craftspeople were plebeians, or common citizens of Rome, and were allowed to vote. Slaves had no rights. The Romans considered slaves the property of their masters. They bought and sold them as servants.

Gladiators were professional fighters who fought one another and wild animals, such as lions and tigers, to the death. They were usually slaves, criminals, or prisoners.

FAMILY LIFE

As head of the family, the father made all the decisions. Education was available to only wealthy families who could afford to hire expensive tutors or send their children to school. Both boys and girls could attend school to learn reading, writing, and mathematics. Between the ages of 10 and 12, girls returned to their mothers, who taught them how to manage the household.

Roman women enjoyed many freedoms and rights. However, they were not allowed to vote or have jobs in the government. Women owned property, worked outside the home, and managed their own businesses.

Leisure and entertainment were important elements of Roman life. Large arenas were constructed for both chariot races and gladiator fights. Other leisure activities included the theatre, public baths, board games, and dinner parties.

*Beginning at age 16, males wore a white **toga** (centre) to show they were adults and could vote. A toga was a loose-fitting robe made from a single piece of cloth. The man and woman show other forms of Roman clothing.*

Society and Culture

RELIGIOUS BELIEFS

The religious beliefs of the Romans were shaped by those of the Greeks and the Etruscans. Like the Greeks, the Romans had twelve gods—six male and six female. Some were imitations of Greek gods. The Romans honoured their gods by building temples, holding festivals, and sacrificing animals in their honour.

The ancient Romans were very superstitious and believed in omens, curses, and spells. An **omen** is an object or event that is believed to bring good or bad luck. The Romans believed that there were spirits everywhere—in fire, water, stones, and even the house. Each day, the head of the family made offerings of food to various household spirits on behalf of the family. The *lares* were another group of spirits who were believed to protect the household. They were the spirits of family ancestors.

Many of the planets in our solar system were named after Roman gods. Can you name them?

❦ Roman Gods ❦

Jupiter	king of the gods and god of the sky and weather
Juno	queen of the gods and goddess of women
Neptune	god of the sea and earthquakes
Minerva	goddess of science and crafts
Ceres	goddess of agriculture
Vesta	goddess of fire
Apollo	god of the sun
Diana	goddess of the moon and hunting
Mercury	god of business and trade
Venus	goddess of love
Vulcan	god of metalworking
Mars	god of war

SOMETHING TO DO

1. Look at the map showing the lands that belonged to ancient Rome on page 61. Work in a small group to compare this map to a current world map. Make a list of the modern names for the countries that were once ruled by Rome.

2. a) What is a *legend*?

   b) In a group, act out the legend of Romulus and Remus. Create a mask for each character in the story.

3. Many Roman gods and goddesses were based on those of ancient Greece. In your notebook, match each Roman god to the Greek god on which he or she is based.

4. Make a chart with the headings Plebeians, Patricians, and Slaves. Compare their roles in Roman society. Consider their occupations and the rights they had.

5. Use books, CD-ROMs, or the Internet to research the importance of Julius Caesar to Rome. Start your research by writing down three questions that you would like to answer with your findings. Consider questions about his actions, his role in government, and his effect on the future of Rome.

Rome

The Romans were able to build on the achievements of the Greeks and the Etruscans to create a mighty empire. As the Roman Empire grew, it gained knowledge from the civilizations it conquered. Many of today's languages, governments, and calendars have their roots in ancient Roman culture. Ancient Roman techniques for construction are still used by people around the world. In fact, some of the actual roads and aqueducts built by the Romans 2000 years ago are still used by people today.

FARMING

As Rome grew in size, food supplies became very important. Wheat, grapes, and olives were grown locally. Bread and wine were the major part of each meal. Olives were an important source of food and oil. The oil was used in lamps, in cooking, and for cleaning the body.

The Romans improved farming equipment. Plows not only cut into the soil, but also turned it over. The Romans also invented the *vallus*, which was a tool, pushed by a mule or donkey, used to cut crops. Before the invention of the vallus, harvesting was done by hand. The Romans also improved hand and water mills used to grind grain. These advancements made it possible for larger amounts of land to be farmed.

Vallus

AQUEDUCTS

The Romans built **aqueducts** to supply towns and villages with fresh water for farming, drinking, and bathing. Aqueducts were stone channels that carried water from its source around and through hills, as well as across valleys, arches, or bridges. These stone channels were covered to prevent the water from being polluted. The Romans built aqueducts throughout their empire, and many can still be found today in England, Spain, France, and Italy. Some still carry water.

ROADS

The Roman Empire was vast, and it was important for armies to move quickly from one battle location to another. To connect the lands that they had conquered, the Romans built thousands of kilometres of roads. These roads were also used by merchants to transport the goods that they traded with people in other parts of the empire. The Romans built their roads so well that they've lasted for more than 2000 years, and some are still in use today.

Roman surveyors first determined the shortest, flattest, and straightest route on which to build a road. They then dug a ditch about a metre deep, which they filled with layers of different-sized stones and cement. The top layer of the road was either gravel or stone slabs. The Romans dug ditches along each side of the road to drain away rainwater, which could destroy it.

This photograph shows the Via Appia in Italy. This 200-km road was completed in 312 BCE.

Roman public bath

ARCHITECTURE

The architectural style of ancient Rome was very similar to that of ancient Greece. Like the Greeks, the ancient Romans used rows of columns and rectangular prisms to build their temples and other structures. During the Roman Empire, the Romans used arches for bridges and aqueducts because they discovered that arches could support a lot of weight. By using arches, the Romans were able to build much larger buildings than the Greeks. By crossing a number of arches, the Romans created the dome roof, which they used in the construction of many buildings, such as temples and public baths. Their architectural techniques can be seen in buildings all around the world today.

Another great discovery of the Romans in the field of building and architecture was that of concrete, which is still an essential building material today. It made construction faster and easier than using stone. Concrete was also very strong, resisted dampness, and was fireproof.

Rome

ART

The artists of ancient Rome admired and often tried to copy the style of the Greek sculptors. They used stone, bronze, and stucco or plaster to create statues of gods, politicians, famous battle scenes, and scenes from everyday life. The **mosaic** was a popular Roman art form. Mosaics are pictures or patterns that are made by cementing together small chips of coloured tile, stone, or marble. Many mosaics tell us a great deal about life in ancient Rome because they show scenes from everyday life.

LANGUAGE

The language of ancient Rome was **Latin**. The Latin alphabet was passed on to the Romans by the Etruscans, who had adapted the alphabet of the Greeks. The alphabets of most modern languages, including English, are based on the Latin alphabet. The ancient Latin alphabet had 23 letters. They are the letters in the English alphabet, except for "j," "u," and "w." Latin became the foundation of the Romance languages, which include French, Spanish, Italian, Portuguese, and Romanian.

About half of the words in the English language come from Latin. Many of these words are in the field of law, for example, *legal*, and science, for example, the word *science* itself. This inscription of Latin appeared on a cloak pin that was made in the 600s BCE. It means "Manius made me for Numerio."

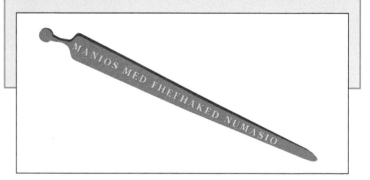

Table VIII

> If a person has maimed another's limb, let the same happen to him unless the matter is settled.

> If he has broken or bruised a freeman's bone with his hand or club, he shall pay 300 bronze coin pieces; if he has broken or bruised a slave's, he shall pay 150.

> If theft has been done at night and the owner kills the thief, it is not against the law. It is forbidden to kill a thief during the day... unless he uses his weapon to fight back, you shall not kill him.

Table XI

> Marriage between plebeians and patricians shall not take place.

LAW AND JUSTICE

Roman law became the basis of many legal systems around the world. The Romans designed their laws to govern the people of Rome and to hold together their vast empire. The first law code of the Romans, the Laws of the 12 Tables, was written in 499 BCE. It dealt with all aspects of Roman life, including wills, property rights, and the behaviour of citizens. Students had to memorize the Laws of the 12 Tables as part of their school work.

Knowledge/Achievements

MATHEMATICS

Roman numerals, the number symbols used by the Romans, are still used in Canada today. Many older buildings show the date they were constructed in Roman numerals. Gravestones, monuments, and the copyright dates of movies, videos, and books are also shown in Roman numerals. Numbers of events, for example, World War II, and monarchs, for example, Henry VIII, also appear in Roman numerals.

The Romans used only seven number symbols in their counting system and did not use zero. They used combinations of these seven symbols to represent numbers. Roman numerals use addition. For example, the number 7 is written as VII (5 + 1 + 1). If a smaller numeral appears before a larger one, it is subtracted from the larger one. This is the case with the numbers 4, 9, 40, and 90. The date 1564 would be written as MDLXIV (1000 + 500 + 50 + 10 + 4).

Roman Number Symbols	Numbers 1 to 10	Other Numbers
I (1)	I (1)	XX (20)
V (5)	II (2)	XXX (30)
X (10)	III (3)	XL (40)
L (50)	IV (4)	LX (60)
C (100)	V (5)	LXX (70)
D (500)	VI (6)	LXXX (80)
M (1000)	VII (7)	XC (90)
	VIII (8)	
	IX (9)	
	X (10)	

CALENDAR

In 45 BCE, Julius Caesar established the Julian calendar. It had 12 months and 365 days, with an additional day added in February every fourth year. In the Julian calendar, the 12 months were Januarius, Februarius, Martius, Aprilis, Maius, Junius, Julius, Augustus, September, October, November, and December. The names of the months are similar to the ones we use today in Canada.

SOMETHING TO DO

1. Create your own version of an ancient Roman mosaic. Cut small squares of coloured construction paper, and arrange them on a large sheet of paper to form a picture or design. Glue the squares to the sheet of paper.

2. a) Can you think of another way that Roman numerals are used today in Canada?

   b) Use Roman numerals to write the number of the present year. Then write the age of each member of your family using Roman numerals.

3. In your opinion, what was the most important contribution of the Romans to modern society? Explain your answer.

4. Do you agree with this statement: "The Romans built on the achievements of the Greeks and the Etruscans"? Explain your answer.

5. Read the Laws of the 12 Tables on page 66. Work with a partner to select one of the laws and debate it. One partner should try to prove that the law is fair. The other one should argue that it is not fair.

9 The Maya

Before creation, there were no people, animals, birds, fish, crabs, trees, or stones. There was only a calm sea. The creators, K'ucumatiz and Tepew, first made the earth and then made animals like deer, jaguar, and snakes. The creators next ordered the animals to speak and praise them for their work, but they could not. The creators decided to make creatures that could. They ground and mixed yellow and white corn. From this cornmeal, they made the first people. People had minds and they could speak, so they worshipped the gods who created them.

(Mayan story describing how people were created)

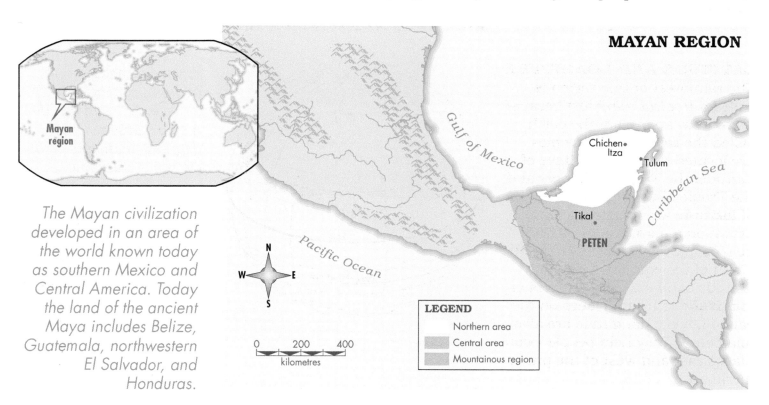

MAYAN REGION

Mayan region

Gulf of Mexico

Chichen Itza

Tulum

Caribbean Sea

Tikal

PETEN

Pacific Ocean

N W E S

0   200   400
kilometres

LEGEND
Northern area
Central area
Mountainous region

The Mayan civilization developed in an area of the world known today as southern Mexico and Central America. Today the land of the ancient Maya includes Belize, Guatemala, northwestern El Salvador, and Honduras.

The forests of the ancient Maya are home to many different types of birds, such as the toucan.

LAND AND CLIMATE

The land of the ancient Maya was rich in natural resources and was home to many different types of wildlife. Plants, birds, animals, and fish provided the Mayan civilization with food and clothing. However, it was not until they cleared the land and grew crops of corn, beans, and squash that the Maya established permanent communities in which to live.

The mountains of the Mayan region contained **basalt**, **jade**, and **obsidian**. The Maya used these types of rock to make sculptures, buildings, religious objects, and the sharp edges of knives and axes. The central area of the Mayan region was covered by dense **rainforests**. A rainforest is a lush forest that receives very heavy rainfall. The climate in this area was hot and humid. The northern area was the driest of the three regions, receiving little rainfall. Grasses, shrubs, and cactus were some of the main types of vegetation in this area.

LATITUDE AND LONGITUDE

The rainforest of this region is called a *tropical rainforest* because it grows in an area of the earth called the **tropics**. The tropics are located between two lines of latitude: the Tropic of Cancer and the Tropic of Capricorn. Lines of **latitude** are imaginary lines drawn on a map or globe. They help people locate places north and south of the equator. Lines of latitude can be used with lines of **longitude** to locate places on the earth. Lines of longitude are also imaginary. They help people locate places east and west of the prime meridian.

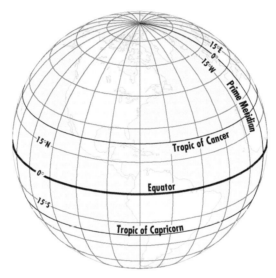

Latitude is measured in degrees, starting from 0° at the equator. Longitude is also measured in degrees, starting at 0° at the prime meridian.

Month	Average Monthly Precipitation (mm)
Jan	88
Feb	76
Mar	46
Apr	40
May	107
June	223
July	165
Aug	166
Sept	295
Oct	314
Nov	250
Dec	243

This chart shows the amount of precipitation that the Mayan rainforest receives on average every month.

SOMETHING TO DO

1. Make a chart to show how the Maya could meet their needs using the natural resources around them. Use the headings Food, Shelter, and Clothing.

2. Locate the land of the Maya on a globe or an atlas map. Between which lines of latitude and longitude is it located?

3. a) Use the information in the precipitation chart on this page to draw a bar graph like the one on page 27. Show how many millimetres of precipitation the Mayan rainforest receives on average every month.

   b) Compare your graph with the one on page 27. How is the amount of precipitation in the Mayan rainforest different from that of Nubia?

The Maya

circa (around) **1000** BCE
Early Mayan Settlements
Settlers looking for fertile land form
the earliest Mayan villages.

300–925 CE
Mayan Golden Age
Mayan civilization experiences
greatest growth.

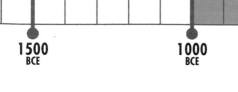

1500 BCE — 1000 BCE — 500 BCE — Year 1 — 500 CE — 100 CE

600 BCE**–300** CE
Larger Mayan Settlements
Mayan villages grow into towns,
then cities, and finally city-states.
The Maya begin to build pyramids.

DID YOU KNOW?

The ruler of a Mayan city-state was considered so important that a cloth was placed in front of his face so that people wouldn't speak to him directly.

HISTORY

Around 1000 BCE, the Maya lived in small villages and gathered food from the forest. They also grew squash, corn, beans, avocados, and chili peppers.

Larger Mayan settlements began to appear around 600 BCE, and by about 250 CE, the Maya formed several city-states that contained temple pyramids, houses, palaces, terraces, and public squares. In the fields, farmers grew corn, fruits, vegetables, cotton, and cocoa.

The Mayan civilization accomplished its greatest achievements between 300 and 925 CE.

GOVERNMENT

Early Mayan settlements were small, and people made decisions through discussion. As communities grew into city-states with large populations, there was a need for greater leadership.

By about 300 CE, each city-state was ruled by a **halach uinic**. He was both the religious and government leader of the community. The halach uinic had absolute power and was born into his position. The Council of State advised the halach uinic on important decisions. The halach uinic selected the members of the Council of State, and often they were his relatives.

Tikal was one of the largest Mayan city-states. Its ruins are located in present-day Guatemala.

SOCIAL STRUCTURE

Because he was the government and religious leader of a city-state, the halach uinic was considered the most important person in Mayan society. He, along with the nobles who advised him, held most of the community's wealth and power. The nobles controlled government, warfare, and trading. Priests were also respected members of society because they performed religious ceremonies and educated young males of the nobility. The common people included craftspeople and traders, but the majority were farmers who lived outside the city-state close to their fields. Slaves either were born into their position or were criminals or prisoners of war. Their chores included doing heavy construction work and transporting goods for trade.

FAMILY LIFE

Entire Mayan families—children, parents, and grandparents—lived together and contributed to the household chores.

Girls were considered adults at the age of 12 and boys at 14. Boys usually married between the ages of 18 and 20, while girls married at 14.

The common people worked long days to take advantage of the cooler mornings and evenings. After the morning meal, most men went to tend their crops.

Women cooked over fires in a three-sided fireplace, which is still used in some areas of Central America today. They used a grinding stone and a hollowed-out stone table to crush softened corn into a paste. This paste could be cooked into a flat bread called a **tortilla**.

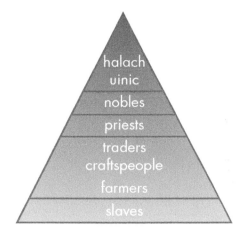

The social structure of the ancient Maya

DID YOU KNOW?

The Maya took great care in their personal appearance and considered a flattened forehead to be a sign of beauty.

Mayan village homes were made up of two rooms that were built on a stone and mud foundation. Walls were made of branches and mud, and the roof was made of thatched palm.

In some parts of Central America, tortillas are still cooked in the traditional Mayan way. In Canada, tortillas can be found in many supermarkets; they can be spread with filling and rolled up.

Society and Culture

This artifact shows a Mayan priest.

RELIGIOUS BELIEFS

Gods and Goddesses

Religion was extremely important to the Maya. Their cities, artwork, wars, games, science, measurement of time, and mathematics were all related to their religious beliefs and rituals. The Maya were *polytheistic*, which means they worshipped many gods and goddesses.

To honour their gods, the Maya held festivals at different times throughout the year. During these festivals, everyone would come to the city-state to say prayers and perform chants and dances for the god or goddess they were honouring. Animals, such as jaguars, turtles, and turkeys, were sacrificed. During natural disasters, such as hurricanes, floods, and earthquakes, humans were sacrificed to make the angry gods happy.

The Maya performed sacrifices and other religious ceremonies in their temples, which they built at the top of stone pyramids.

Afterlife

The Maya believed that there was a heaven and an underworld. When they died, important rulers were buried underneath the city pyramids. They were buried with food, weapons, clothing, jewellery, and servants to serve their needs in the afterlife. Common people were buried below the floor of the family home along with food, drink, and personal items to be used in the afterlife. The family home was then abandoned, and a new one was built somewhere else.

Some of the most important Mayan gods were Itzamna, Ixchel, and Ah Mun.

Itzamna
The supreme being of the earth and sky

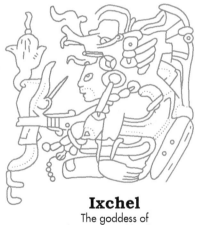

Ixchel
The goddess of the moon and healing

Ah Mun
The god of corn

SOMETHING TO DO

1. The government of the ancient Maya can be considered a theocracy, which is a type of government led by a god or religious figure. Why? What other ancient civilizations in this book can be considered theocracies?

2. How were the beliefs and practices of the ancient Maya regarding the afterlife similar to those of the ancient Egyptians?

3. Corn was an extremely important food to the Maya. They used it to make tamales, tortillas, and atole. Research each of these foods, and explain what they are. Write or illustrate a recipe to describe how they are prepared.

ore archaeological investigation needs to be done to solve the many mysteries of the ancient Mayan civilization. However, the evidence that we now have shows that it was one of the most advanced early civilizations of the Americas. The architectural skills of the Maya made it possible for them to build impressive cities with enormous structures. They were skilled mathematicians and astronomers. The ancient Maya also developed a writing system and extensive trade routes.

ARCHITECTURE

The Maya built **temple-pyramids**, where they worshipped and participated in religious ceremonies. Important structures, such as temples, were built on top of pyramids and painted on both the inside and outside. The Maya built large step pyramids using limestone and cement. These pyramids had steps on one or more sides leading up to the temple at the top. Within these temples, there were highly decorated altars where priests performed sacrifices and other religious ceremonies. Sometimes the bodies of Mayan rulers were buried beneath the pyramids.

TRADE

Trade was very important to the Mayan civilization. The Maya developed extensive trade routes, which helped to connect their area together. They used canoes that could hold up to 40 people to transport goods up and down rivers. People who lived along the coast traded cocoa, rubber, and salt. They transported their goods inland along rivers and streams to settlements in the forests and mountains. The people who lived in the forests grew vegetables, such as corn, beans, and squash, which they also transported along the rivers. Those who lived in the mountains mined basalt, sandstone, obsidian, silver, and jade. Jade and silver were used to make jewellery, which the ancient Maya wore and traded. The photograph shows a jade pendant.

DID YOU KNOW?

The Maya were the first people to discover chewing gum. They chewed the tasty hardened sap of the sapodilla evergreen tree. This sap is called *chicle*.

The Maya

WRITING

The Mayan system of writing used hieroglyphic symbols to represent combinations of sounds and ideas. Archaeologists have identified over 800 different Mayan hieroglyphs. They were square with rounded corners, and they were read from top to bottom and left to right. Archaeologists have found Mayan writing on temple altars, walls of public buildings, and pottery. The Maya carved information about important dates and great events in the lives of their rulers on large stone monuments called **stelae**. They also painted hieroglyphs onto sheets of paper made of fig-tree bark. The Maya joined these sheets together to make books called **codices**.

PAINTING AND POTTERY

The Maya used a variety of paints to colour the inside and outside of their buildings, decorate their pottery, and create artwork. To make paint colours, they used different plants and minerals. Their favourite colour was blue, made from the indigo plant. They made red using iron oxide or rust, yellow from the mineral ochre, brown from asphalt or bitumen, and black from carbon or ashes.

The Maya made clay utensils such as cups, plates, pots, bowls, vases, and other containers. They also made statues of gods and goddesses.

MATHEMATICS

The Maya used combinations of three symbols to represent numbers: the dot had a value of one, the horizontal bar had a value of five, and the shell represented zero. Some historians believe that the Maya may have been the first ancient civilization to use zero. They used combinations of these symbols to represent numbers up to 19.

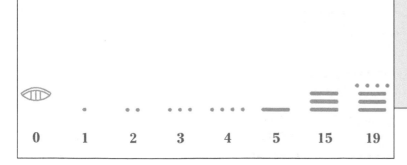

| 0 | 1 | 2 | 3 | 4 | 5 | 15 | 19 |

ASTRONOMY

The Maya believed that time was under the control of the gods. It was therefore important for priests to determine when good or evil gods were going to be in control of time. The Maya built observatories from which priests studied the sky and the positions of the sun, the moon, and the planets very closely. Their observations were so precise that they could predict eclipses. They calculated the length of the year to be 365.2420 days, which is extremely close to the 365.2422 days of our current calendar.

The Maya developed three calendars: the *Tzolkin*, which was used to plan religious feasts and festivals; the *Haab*, which was the 365-day farming calendar; and the *Long Count*, which was used to mark very long time spans.

SOMETHING TO DO

1. Complete a chart like the one below to compare the pyramids of the Maya with those of Egypt and the ziggurats of Mesopotamia.

	Mayan Pyramids	Ziggurats of Mesopotamia	Pyramids of Egypt
Use			
Materials Used			
Appearance			

2. a) Use the Mayan number system to write the numbers from 10 to 19.

   b) Create your own number system using your own symbols. Illustrate your number system from 1 to 19 on a large sheet of paper. Be prepared to present your number system to the class.

3. Use books, the Internet, CD-ROMs, or other resources to find out more information about one of the three calendars used by the Maya. Write a brief description.

4. Use Plasticine or clay to make a model of a piece of Mayan pottery. Show your item to the class and describe how it could be used in Mayan society.

5. Many Canadian tourists visit southern Mexico and Belize every year and have seen Mayan ruins. To find out more about the cities and architecture of the Maya, invite a person who has visited these sites to come and speak to your class. Perhaps the guest will have slides, photos, or a video to show you as well.

10 Canadian Civilization

How have the civilizations of the ancient world contributed to our society? Canada is a civilization that includes many cultures. Its history, government, social structure, religious beliefs, and achievements have their origins in civilizations that existed thousands of years ago. Some of these civilizations you have studied in this book. There are many others, including the civilizations of Aboriginal peoples that you have learned about in other studies. As Canada continues to grow as a civilization, our appreciation of the contributions of early civilizations to our way of life will continue to be an important part of that growth.

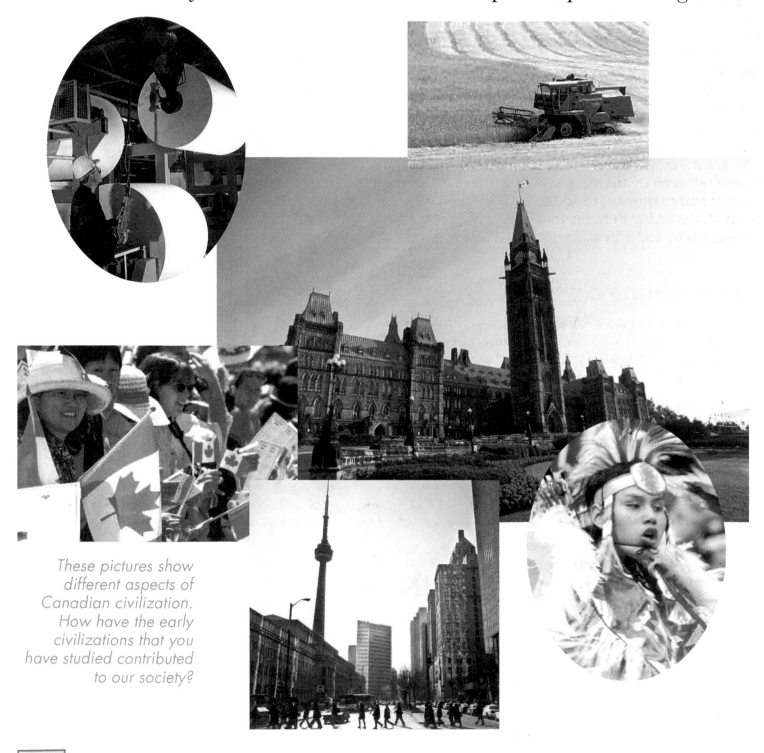

These pictures show different aspects of Canadian civilization. How have the early civilizations that you have studied contributed to our society?

CANADA AND ANCIENT CIVILIZATIONS

Like the government of ancient Greece, the government of Canada is a democracy that recognizes the rights and personal freedoms of every person. Our federal government is centralized in Ottawa. So is our civil service. The idea of centralized government and a trained civil service came from ancient China, where the government was concentrated in the city of Changan during the Qin dynasty.

Female leaders were rare in ancient times. In the Kush civilization, African women had important roles within government, and this opportunity exists in Canada today.

Many resources and technologies first used by the peoples of early civilizations are used by Canadians today in their homes, businesses, and cities. The Maya grew and produced cotton, cocoa, chewing gum, and rubber, which are all used in Canada today. The wheel was invented in Mesopotamia and is now found in thousands of everyday objects in Canada and around the world. Many surgical instruments and techniques, including plastic surgery, which doctors practise all around the world today, were first developed in ancient India.

The ancient Romans designed and constructed roads to transport people and trade goods, as well as aqueducts to transport water. We use their techniques to build roads and transport water today. The earliest form of paper was developed in ancient Egypt. It was called *papyrus*, from which we got the word *paper*. Today paper is a necessity in our lives, and the paper industry is an important part of the Canadian economy.

SOMETHING TO DO

1. On an outline map of the world, draw and label the civilizations studied in this book. Use a different colour for each civilization, and write the names of the oceans, the equator, the Tropic of Cancer, and the Tropic of Capricorn.

2. In your opinion, what are the three most important contributions of early civilizations to the world? Explain your answer. Be prepared to share your answer with the class.

3. Work with a partner to select one of the early civilizations presented in this book. Choose one aspect of this civilization, for example, family life, government, or religion, and dramatize it in a radio play that you record on a cassette or videotape. Present your cassette or video to the class.

4. Choose two early civilizations and use a chart to compare their governments, social structures, religious beliefs, and family lives. How can you explain the similiarities between the two cultures? How can you explain the differences?

Glossary

acupuncture an ancient Chinese method to heal pain and sickness using special needles that are inserted into the skin at certain points on the body

Aesop's fables short stories, written by a slave in ancient Greece named Aesop, that teach a lesson and often have animals as the main characters

afterlife the continuation of a person's soul or spirit after his or her body dies

alphabet the letters or symbols used to represent the sounds of a language

amulets charms used to keep evil away

agriculture farming; cultivating land, growing crops, and raising farm animals

ancestor worship prayers and offerings for family members who have died

anthropomorphic having human form or characteristics

aqueduct structures that are used to transport water from one place to another

archaeologists scientists who study the way ancient peoples lived

archaeology the study of ancient peoples and their cultures through remains and artifacts

artifacts objects made by people

Aryans warlike people who travelled in tribes around the grasslands of Asia and Europe

Assembly a group of people gathered together for political or religious reasons

Aswan Dam a dam built in 1961 on the Nile River to provide Egypt with electrical power and water all year round

Athens a city-state in ancient Greece; the capital city of modern-day Greece

barter system a method of trading by exchanging one product or service for another

basalt dark, dense volcanic rock

BCE Before Common Era; used in place of BC (before Christ) to refer to dates prior to year 1

bronze a metal created by combining copper and tin

Buddhism a religion started in India based on the ideas of the Buddha, who believed that all people are equal and that everyone should be kind to all living things

calligraphy the art of beautiful handwriting

canopic jars containers used in ancient Egypt to hold the internal organs of a mummified body

caravans groups of people travelling together across a desert or on a long journey

cardinal points the four main points of the compass: north, south, east, and west

castes the separate social classes that people are divided into according to the strict social structure of India

cataracts small waterfalls

CE Common Era; used in place of AD to refer to dates after, and including, year 1

citizens people who belong to a community

city-states large cities, and their surrounding territory, with their own government

civilization a community of people living in permanent settlements, such as villages, towns, or cities, who have developed knowledge in such areas as farming, trade, government, art, law, and science

civil service a group of government workers

climate the weather conditions of an area over a long period of time

codices ancient writings in book form

Confucianism a philosophy based on the ideas of Confucius, an ancient Chinese philosopher who believed in an orderly society in which everyone has a role, place, and responsibility

contour interval the difference in height between contour lines

contour lines lines on a map that connect places of the same elevation or height

Council an assembly of people who can provide advice or govern

culture the beliefs, arts, and customs of a particular group of people; a way of life

cuneiform wedge-shaped symbols used to represent objects and ideas; the written language of ancient Mesopotamia

delta the flat, triangle-shaped area of land at the mouth of a river where silt is deposited

democracy a type of government in which people have a say in how they are governed

dictator a ruler who has total control over a government and its people

dictatorship a government controlled by a dictator

domesticate to tame animals to live with people and be used for farm work or food

dynasty a series of rulers belonging to the same family

economy a nation's wealth

elevation the height of land above sea level

emperor a ruler of a large region, or number of regions, who has total control

Etruscans people who lived north of Rome and conquered the Romans around 600 BCE

excavation the digging up of remains or ancient artifacts

Fertile Crescent an arc-shaped band of land that stretches from the Persian Gulf to the Mediterranean Sea

feudal system the rule of a community by local lords and nobles who report to the king

flood plains low, flat areas of land along the banks of a river that are easily flooded

gladiators professional fighters who were forced to fight other people and wild animals for the entertainment of others

government the group of people who rule a nation

granary a storehouse for grain

Great Wall of China a 2200-km wall built in ancient China during the Zhou and Qin dynasties to keep out invaders

guru a teacher or instructor in India

halach uinic a Mayan ruler who was born into his position and was both a religious and a government leader

hieroglyphs a system of writing developed in ancient Egypt that used pictures to represent words and sounds

Hinduism a religion based on the original beliefs of the Aryans who settled in India; the main religion of India

Hippocratic oath a promise made by doctors to treat their patients to the best of their ability

history the study of past events

human features things built or created by people to change the face of the earth, for example, roads, cities, and country borders

Iliad an adventure story in the form of a poem, by the Greek writer Homer, that tells about the Trojan War

Indus Valley civilization a community that developed along the Indus and Sarasvati rivers around 2500 BCE; also called the *Harappa culture*

intermediate points the points between the four main points of the compass: northeast, northwest, southeast, and southwest

irrigation the supplying of water for land

Italian peninsula a boot-shaped piece of land that extends into the Mediterranean Sea; present-day country of Italy

jade a green stone used for decorative and religious purposes in many cultures

kandake a Nubian queen or female ruler

kareze a method of irrigation in which tunnels are dug into the ground until the water table is found

Latin the language of ancient Rome

latitude (lines of) imaginary horizontal lines drawn on a map above and below the equator

legalism a philosophy in ancient China that required all people to follow the laws of the land and obey those in authority

legend a key explaining the symbols found on a map; a story from the past that people believe to be true

legion the largest unit of the ancient Roman army; made up of between 4000 and 6000 soldiers

longitude (lines of) imaginary lines drawn on a map running from the North Pole to the South Pole

Lower Nile the section of the Nile River that stretches north from the first cataract to the Mediterranean Sea

map grid a system of numbers and letters that helps to locate a place on a map

Meroitic the written language of the ancient Nubians

Minoan the earliest civilization of ancient Greece, located on the island of Crete

monarchy a government headed by a king or queen

monsoons seasonal winds of the Indian Ocean and south Asian region that blow from the southwest (wet season) in the summer and northeast (dry season) in the winter

mosaic Roman art form in which pictures or designs are created by cementing in place small chips of coloured tile, stone, or marble

Mount Olympus a mountain in northern Greece that was considered the home of Greek gods and goddesses

mummification a process used in ancient Egypt to preserve a dead body, which included wrapping it in linen bandages

Mycenae a powerful civilization on the mainland of ancient Greece

myths stories about gods and heroes that are sometimes used to explain life and creation

natural harbours sheltered areas along a coastline that provide protection for boats

Neolithic Age the time period between 8000 and 5000 BCE when people switched from hunting and gathering food to producing their own food by farming

Nile the longest river in the world, located in northeast Africa

nomadic moving from place to place in search of food

obsidian glass-like volcanic rock used by the Maya as a cutting tool

Odyssey a story in the form of a poem, by the ancient Greek writer Homer, about King Odysseus and his many adventures

Olympic Games a festival of athletic events that originated in ancient Greece and takes place every four years

Glossary

omen an event that foretells what will happen in the future

oracles people who can read and explain signs from the gods

papyrus the earliest form of paper made from the papyrus reeds that grew along the banks of the Nile River in ancient Egypt

parmanu the name given to atoms by an ancient Indian philosopher named Kanada

patricians members of the wealthy, land-owning class of ancient Rome

pharaoh the title given to the rulers of ancient Egypt

philosophers people who study ideas about science, law, human emotions, good, and evil

physical features natural formations that make up the surface of the earth, such as rivers, mountains, lakes, and deserts

plebeians members of the common class in ancient Rome

polytheism the worship of more than one god

precipitation all types of moisture that fall from the sky, for example, rain or snow

provinces conquered lands of the ancient Romans; political regions of a country

pyramids large buildings made of stone with a square base and sloping sides meeting at a central point; used for religious purposes by the ancient Egyptians, Nubians, and Maya

qi according to the ancient Chinese, it is the energy that flows through the universe and must not be disturbed

rainforest a dense forest growing in an area of heavy rainfall

republic a democratic form of government in which people vote for their leaders

reservoir dam a place where water is collected and stored for irrigation

Sanskrit the language of the Aryans used in the religious writings of ancient India

sarcophagus a decorated coffin, often painted with the dead person's face

scribes people in ancient civilizations who could read and write; they usually worked for the government or in temples

Senate the highest level of government where decisions and recommendations are made; the group of wealthy men who governed ancient Rome

shaduf an irrigation tool used in ancient Egypt to lift water from a lower to a higher level

Silk Road an ancient trade route that was 6400 km long between China and the Mediterranean Sea

silt fine sand or particles of soil carried in a river

smelted heated rock to remove the metals that are in it, for example, copper, iron, and tin

Sparta a military city-state of ancient Greece

stelae large stone monuments on which important information was carved

Taoism a philosophy based on the ideas of Lao-tzu, who believed that life should be in harmony with nature

Ta-Seti a civilization that developed in Nubia between 3800 and 3100 BCE

temple-pyramids Mayan structures built at the top of enormous stone pyramids where religious ceremonies were performed

theocracy a government ruled by a religious leader

Tiber River a river in Italy; the civilization of ancient Rome developed along its banks

timeline a line that shows important dates and events in history and can be used to show the development of a civilization

toga a loose-fitting robe made of a single piece of cloth

tortilla a flat bread made from cornmeal or wheat flour

tributaries streams or rivers that flow into a larger river or lake

tropics the region of the earth between the Tropic of Cancer and Tropic of Capricorn

tumulus tomb a Nubian grave in the form of a large mound made of earth and stone

untouchables a class of people in Hindu society who were considered lowly and "unclean"

Upper Nile the section of the Nile River that stretches south of the first cataract to the rivers of the White and Blue Nile

vizier the second in command after the pharaoh in ancient Egyptian society

Yangtze River called *Chang Jiang He* in Chinese, it is the longest river in China

Yellow River called *Huang He* in Chinese, it is located in northern China; Chinese civilization developed along its banks

yin and yang a Chinese symbol that represents the opposite forces in nature in harmony with each other

Zeus the supreme ruler of all Greek gods and goddesses

ziggurat a Mesopotamian temple with a pyramid-shaped base built to house the gods when they visit the earth